# Shaped

## by Saints

### by Devi Mukherjee

With Durga Smallen
and Swami Kriyananda

Crystal Clarity, Publishers
Nevada City, California

Cover and book design by C. A. Starner Schuppe

Photographs by Devi Mukherjee, Durga Smallen, and
Swami Kriyananda

ISBN: 1-56589-149-X


Printed in the United States of America

2   4   6   8   10   9   7   5   3   1


Crystal

Clarity


**Crystal Clarity, Publishers**
14618 Tyler-Foote Road
Nevada City, CA 95959-8599

Phone: 800-424-1055 or 530-478-7600
Fax: 530-478-7610
E-mail: clarity@crystalclarity.com
Website: www.crystalclarity.com

# Dedication

I bow at the lotus feet of my Beloved Divine Mother, Master Krishna, Jesus Christ, Babaji, Lahiri Mahasaya, Sri Yukteswar Giri, beloved Paramhansa Yogananda, and the saints of all religions. Also to Anandamoyee Ma, Narayan Swami, Kailash Pati, Rani Mata, and many Himalayan masters and swamis; and lastly to Swami Atmananda, Daya Mata, Swami Kriyananda, and Tulsi Bose.

Paramhansa Yogananda in 1926

# Contents

Foreword . . . . . . . . . . . . . . . . . . . . . . . . . .6
Introduction . . . . . . . . . . . . . . . . . . . . . . . .9
1. I Find My Guru . . . . . . . . . . . . . . . . . . . .12
2. A Trek in the Himalayas . . . . . . . . . . . . . . .24
3. A Visit from Mt. Washington . . . . . . . . . . . .31
4. An Official Visit from SRF . . . . . . . . . . . . . .41
5. Tulsi Bose, Yogananda's Boyhood Friend . . .48
6. Ranchi—Then, a Trek to Badrinath! . . . . . . .57
7. Pilgrimage to South India . . . . . . . . . . . . . .71
8. A Yogi Encounters Modern Science . . . . . . .77
9. Fright from a Cobra! . . . . . . . . . . . . . . . . .83
10. God in Organizations: God in Our Souls . . .97
11. A New Flowering? . . . . . . . . . . . . . . . . . .108
12. No Tibet This Time . . . . . . . . . . . . . . . . .116
13. The Travelers Return . . . . . . . . . . . . . . . .124

# Foreword

## by Durga Smallen

I met Devi Mukherjee for the first time in the Fall of 1986. My husband and I were leading a pilgrimage to India with our long-time friends and *gurubhais,*\* David and Asha Praver. Our spiritual teacher, Swami Kriyananda, had told us stories about Devi. They had been brother monks together in Yogoda Satsanga Society (YSS), the Indian branch of Self-Realization Fellowship (SRF). The two organizations were founded by our guru, Paramhansa Yogananda. Devi had joined YSS in India, and Swamiji had joined SRF at Mt. Washington, Los Angeles, the international headquarters. They met in Calcutta in October, 1958, and both lived in the YSS ashrams until Kriyananda left SRF in 1962.

Devi, his wife Hassi (pronounced Hashi), and their son Manash now live in Calcutta and serve as the meditation group leaders of Ananda, the organization founded by Swami Kriyananda in 1968. Devi and his family are deep and sincere devotees of Paramhansa Yogananda, and dear friends of us at Ananda who know them. Their dedication to God and Guru, and also their divine friendship for Kriyananda, is deeply inspiring.

Devi and Hassi live in the home of Yogananda's

---

\*Brothers and sisters in the family of the same guru, or spiritual teacher.

close boyhood friend, Tulsi Bose, Hassi's father, and keep their home open twenty-four hours a day to anyone who wishes to meditate in the rooms where Yogananda meditated, and also Anandamoyee Ma, Sri Yukteswarji, Balaram Bose (a direct disciple of Sri Ramakrishna Paramhansa), Swami Vivek-ananda, and other great saints.

This is Devi's story of the great men and women he has met during forty-five years of spiritual seeking. As we interviewed him about details in his book, tears constantly came into his eyes as he relived those thrilling scenes.

In the *Mahabharata* (one of the great spiritual epics of India), Lord Krishna tells his disciple, Uddhava, to go to the Himalayas and meditate on Him. For thousands of years, pilgrims have done likewise, braving the dangers of snow, narrow mountain paths, and wild animals to reach the great temples there, dedicated to the worship of God. Devi, possessed of a keen desire to make these pilgrimages, met saintly people and had extraordinary experiences in their presence, experiences that bestowed on him deep soul peace and a sense of inner fulfillment.

When I asked Devi why he had wanted to make these long treks, he replied, "I wanted to meditate in holy places, and I wanted my life to be shaped by saints."

He met God-realized beings in, and outside, the small villages that are the heart of that amazing land of sages and saints whose lives are far removed from what most people consider the "normal"—the hubbub and bustle of daily commerce.

As he states in his book, however, "Even though I had met a few highly advanced yogis in my travels, up to January, 1955, I never felt an inclination to accept a guru." In that month it was that he met his own destined guru, once-living in form but now in formlessness, Paramhansa Yogananda.

I hope you enjoy Devi's book as much as I have. You will come to know this man as much through his vibrations as through the story he relates. I hope that you, too, will be impressed and grateful for the example of his moment-to-moment focus on the divine, which turns many a prospective disaster into a divine blessing.

Durga Smallen

# Introduction

I was born in North Calcutta on 20th March, 1927, at my family's home. When I was six months old my father died, and my mother was obliged to leave our home owing to certain problems with our property. Mother and I went to live in the home of my mother's brother in South Calcutta.

At seventeen, a close friend and I joined the army. In the end we joined the resistance movement against British rule, and were eventually jailed for five months. After my release in 1945, I was accepted into Ashutosh College, where, in 1947 (the year India won its independence from Great Britain), I received my B.A. degree. From 1949 to 1954, I was employed as a refrigeration engineer, and in that capacity was sent throughout India. Thus, perhaps, began my "career" as a traveller!

During that period of my life I had very few friends. My mind could not accept wine, dancing, smoking, and other so-called "pleasures" of youth, so I kept to myself much of the time. My mother arranged for me to marry when I was twenty-eight, but, having no desire for marriage, I declined.

In 1966, during a visit to the great woman saint Anandamoyee Ma, I received an answer from her to my burning question: "Should I live the rest of my life in Himalayan solitude?"

"You cannot do so," she said. "You will have to return and enter family life. Your wife, however, will belong to Yogananda's spiritual family, and will herself be a devotee." Another great saint, Kailash Pati, with whom I stayed in Ranikhet, a Himalayan town, told me the same thing later on.

I had already met Hassi, my wife to be, on 4th May in 1955 at the Yogoda Satsanga Society ashram outside Calcutta, but had had no interest in marrying at that time. In 1969, however, on 3rd February, we were finally married. Our son Manash was born 4th January, 1970. I am my mother's only son, and Manash also is my and Hassi's only son.

Manash, Hassi, and me

# Shaped by Saints

# I Find My Guru

On 1st January, 1955, I was getting ready to leave the house to play soccer with a few friends. I picked up the local newspaper to see if the day's outdoor activities were listed. I was very interested at that time in all kinds of sports, soccer being my favorite.

As I started to open the paper, I beheld a very attractive photo on the first page. Beneath it were the words, "On 5th January, Paramhansa Yogananda's birthday will be held at Yogoda Math, Dakshineswar." My mind was suddenly attracted to this photo. Instead of going to the soccer game, I left at once for Dakshineswar.

On my way to the address given in the paper, I stopped first at the Kali Temple in Dakshineswar, which had been made famous by Sri Ramakrishna Paramhansa, one of the great masters of the Nineteenth century, and, among all saints up to then, my "first love." I used often to go there and meditate, tuning in to the power and blessings of the great Master, Sri Ramakrishna, which still permeate that holy place. God's presence was, to me, more palpable there than anywhere else.

After some time, I quietly left and made my way to nearby Yogoda Math. On entering the prayer room in the main building, I was struck by four large, beautiful pictures of masters I didn't recognize. Their names, I learned subsequently, were Babaji, Lahiri Mahasaya, Sri Yukteswar Giri, and Paramhansa Yogananda. Who they were I had no idea at the time, but I was amazed that here in this place so near Calcutta I would behold images of such radiant beings that were completely unknown to me. My mind instantly responded, "This is a good place to be. Remain a while longer."

I walked around the ashram, and was met by a dynamic and powerful man with a kindly face and a benign smile. He introduced himself as Swami Atmananda. Later I learned that he was the secretary and *dharmacharya* of Yogoda Satsanga Society, and as such had authority from Yogananda to train others in the principles of *Sanatan Dharma*, the "eternal religion," ancient name of the Hindu religion. He traveled all over India in service to this cause. Later I learned that Yogananda discovered him when Atmananda was eleven years old, through a mutual friend of theirs, Tulsi Bose.

He, in turn, introduced me to Jim Wood from America; two German boys, Eitel and Prell; a very nice boy from Switzerland, Habluz; and to other swamis and brahmacharis of the ashram as well.

Jim Wood was the talkative one of the group. He

told me about Paramhansa Yogananda, their guru. Even though I had met a few highly advanced yogis in my travels, until now I had never been drawn to accepting anyone as my guru. Jim Wood asked if I had read Yogananda's *Autobiography of a Yogi*. I replied I had not, so he offered me a copy of the book in Bengali, commenting, "You will find everything about the Master in there."

How they all impressed me! In their shining simplicity, I thought, it was obvious that they led their lives guided by divine teachings. What was their secret? Obviously, again, it had to be that they had a true master! I wondered, Why have I not had this good fortune? How I would have loved to be in their shoes! Soon I learned that Yogananda had had his *mahasamadhi* (a great yogi's final exit from the body) only three years earlier, on March 7th, 1952. Gazing into these men's eyes, I felt they had something that I, too, wanted. Being with them increased my zeal for the Divine.

As the day advanced, Jim Wood took me to the dining room, where the monks had gathered for their midday meal. Swami Atmananda told us a few miraculous stories of Yogananda's life. (The Master's life seemed to me to have been one long miracle!) Swami Atmananda (or "Swamiji," as I learned to call him) then invited me to attend the celebration on 5th January in commemoration of the Master's birthday. This was four days from then. I accepted with alacrity. As I returned home, it was with eager anticipation of the coming event.

That day dawned, and I left home for the ashram in Dakshineswar, arriving earlier than most of the guests, who came at last in great numbers. I spent the entire day there. The most wonderful part of the celebration was watching my newly made friends take their *brahmacharya* (renunciation) vows. Jim Wood took the name *Brahmachari Paramananda.* The Swiss boy, Habluz, took the name *Gyanananda,* meaning "Bliss through divine wisdom."

As I left the ashram later that evening, my mind was overflowing with joy. The Master was in my mind the whole time. My thoughts kept repeating, "He is the one for you. It would be absurd to look anywhere else!"

Swami Atmanandaji and Paramananda both told me to come every Sunday for *satsanga* (spiritual fellowship) and have lunch with them after the service. I soon found myself going there almost weekly to

Paramananda in 1957

join the seven dedicated monks who lived there together.

We honored Yogananda's *mahasamadhi* on 7th March of that year by meditating all night, from 4:00 in the afternoon until 10:00 the next morning. For me it was an amazing experience. I'd been part of this group only three months. Atmanandaji had taught me basic techniques of meditation during one of my first visits to the ashram, but I never thought I'd be able to meditate so long. Yet the "effort" proved effortless! I reflected, it certainly must have been the Master's grace. Meditation has remained my life-practice ever since.

Afterwards, we were given *prasad* of blessed sweets. Then Atmanandaji invited me to come on 4th May for his own birthday. It astonished me that one thousand devotees and disciples attended that event.

Being in the ashram, above all during meditation there, I came to appreciate who Atmanandaji was: a man who cared deeply for all who came to him; fearless, kind, and overflowing with love. He always gave to his guru any thanks we expressed for what he'd given us, and whenever he spoke to us of Yogananda, tears filled his eyes. His familiarity with the divine teachings was deeply inspiring to me. I drew from him all that I could.

Swamiji ("ji" implies a note of respect) had come onto this path in 1935 when he received *diksha* (spiritual initiation) from Paramhansa Yogananda. He was born Prakash Das, but after taking Kriya initiation was known as Prakash Brahmachari. It wasn't until 1953 when he became a swami that he was called Swami Atmananda. Swamiji grew up in Calcutta and in his early adult years operated an harmonium and piano business, Das & Co., with his father. As they were quite well-to-do, Swamiji was able to devote all his later years to bringing souls to God.

Swamiji had given me a meditation technique known as *yoti mudra* on my first arrival. This is a technique by which the meditator can behold the inner light and through it become aware of the presence of God. Swamiji used to talk to the disciples every morning and evening about this path—its techniques of meditation, its way of life, the attitudes a devotee ought to develop. I had never before known peace like this. We were irresistibly drawn to Swamiji's deep devotion to God and Guru. Inevitably, he was deeply loved in return by all those around him.

He was also an inspiring singer, and often chanted with us. It was, indeed, through music that he taught best.

Meanwhile, I had finished reading *Autobiography of a Yogi*. It made me think of the *Bhagavad Gita:* It was scripture. Even today, it is the only book I read. Someone once asked me if I believed in the miracles described in it. All I could say in reply was, "I have seen many miracles myself in the Himalayas. Advanced yogis can do anything they want." As a saint whom I often visited high in the Himalayas would say, "Past, present, future: It's all the same!"

I did not know at the time that my own mother was a *Kriyaban* (practitioner of *Kriya Yoga*, the highest technique of meditation), nor that she had already read *Autobiography of a Yogi* many years earlier. It was only when she realized how serious I was becoming about these teachings that she told me she had taken the holy Kriya initiation, through Panchanon Bhattacharya,* a direct and highly advanced disciple of Lahiri Mahasaya, Yogananda's *param-param* guru, or guru's guru. Yogananda called him "Bhattacharya Mahasaya." (*Mahasaya* means "great-souled." To this day a picture of him hangs in Yogananda's meditation room at his boyhood home at 4 Garpar Road.)

From the time I was six years old until the beginning of World War II my mother went often by train on the several-hour journey it took to reach Panchanon's lovely ashram, where he lived with his disciples. The ashram was situated on seventeen acres of land in Deoghar, a small town in the state of Bihar about 170 miles northeast of Calcutta. As I was only a small boy, I would play outside while she sat, absorbed in his spirit. Unfortunately, I didn't realize at the time that my mother was in the presence of a great saint!

Now, twenty years later, she told me miracles of his life. She said that many times while visiting her

---

*Panchanon Bhattacharya was one of the three disciples of Lahiri Mahasaya who witnessed the manifestation of the great guru's physical form after he'd left his body in death.

guru, Babaji (the first, still-living, in our line of gurus) would come visit him also! In fact, Babaji came to give Bhattacharya instructions—using him, as she put it, as his secretary!*

"Don't come tomorrow," Bhattacharyaji would tell disciples who wanted to see him. "I shall be busy with Babaji."

\* \* \* \* \*

It soon became clear that there was something here, in the YSS order, for me. My mind tried to tell me to go back to my familiar world, but my heart kept repeating, almost like a mantra, "Stay with them." Finally I packed up my few belongings, left home and job, and joined Yogoda Satsanga Society. This was in May, 1955. My two closest friends in the order, Paramananda and Gyanananda, were very happy. I took Kriya Yoga initiation from Atmanandaji, and he advised me to stay with them at our nearby Baranagore Ashram.† I lived there for a year, after which I transferred to the main *math* (monastery) in Dakshineswar.

On 5th January, 1956, I took the vows of *brahmacharya* and the name *Karunananda,* which

---

*By "secretary" is meant, one assumes, someone who could produce for him some spiritual treatise, as in the case of Sri Yukteswar, whom he asked to write the book, *The Holy Science;* or one who could carry out certain tasks for him, just as when he gave Master instructions and advice regarding his work.

†At that time, YSS had two ashrams outside Calcutta not far from each other. In 1961, however, the Baranagore ashram was sold.

means "bliss through compassion." Also, on this day I met other disciples of Master: Tulsi Bose (Yogananda's boyhood friend who took Kriya initiation from him at the age of twenty); Tulsi's wife, Martan Ma;* Tulsi's father Hari Narayan, or, as Master called him, "Baba Mahasaya." (*Baba* means "father"; *Mahasaya* means, as I have said, "great souled.") Other relatives I met that day were two cousins of Master's, Prabhas Ghose and Prakash; Ramakrishna Ghosh (who became known to us as Gagan-da†), who was the son of Master's elder brother Ananta, and lived in Serampore;‡ Sananda

After my *brahma-charya* vows in 1956

* *Martan* is the highest expression of the term, Mother. Master gave her that name, and always called her that.

†*The suffix, "da,"* means "elder brother." I called him, simply, "Da" as a term of affection. I felt toward him this sense of familial closeness.

‡Its original name, which is still used by the people of the town, was *Sri Ram Pur*, which means, "City of Lord Rama." It wasn't until much later, in 1961 in Serampore, that I got to meet Gagan's wife Meera. Master had not only picked her out as the

and Bishnu Ghosh, Master's younger brothers; Thamu-di,* Master's younger sister; and many others.

Every Sunday, and on other special occasions, I traveled the seven miles to Dakshineswar. Eventually I came to regard all of these people as not only Master's family, but as my own family as well.

Swami Atmananda, who had known Gagan since 1910, loved the devotion with which he sang, and would announce with great enthusiasm, "Gagan will lead the singing today!" Gagan-da had one of the sweetest, most melodious voices I have ever heard. I soon became one of his greatest admirers, and would ask him to sing those of Master's chants that I knew, and that he himself particularly loved, such as "Will That Day Come to Me, Ma?," "He Hari Sundara! (O God Beautiful!)" and other songs to Divine Mother Kali. He would sing for hours at a time. How his voice thrilled me! I would say to him, "Oh, Da, let us *sing!*" Whenever he sang, he forgot even food.

Many stories of Master were told the day I took my vows. Thamu-di, Master's sister, described a

---

ideal wife for Gagan, but had also performed the wedding ceremony himself, in 1936. Over two thousand people had attended the ceremony! I found her sweet, compassionate, and completely devoted to God and Guru. Martan and Meera Ghosh were very good friends, and to this day Meera and I have a deep and sincere friendship in God.

* *"Di"* is a suffix signifying "older sister," which of course she was in relation to us, though she was younger than Master.

21

literally haunting event that had happened to her as a young girl:

"One day, Mejda (the name Master's brothers and sisters called him; it means, 'second-eldest brother') lost a set of golden buttons inlaid with diamond fittings, given him by our father and for that reason precious to him. Mejda was with his friends Tulsi-da and Prakash Das (Atmanandaji), and asked them what they thought he should do about it. Tulsi-da suggested that he call forth a spirit and ask it to tell him where the buttons were. Mejda then sent for me and, wanting to use me to find the buttons, hypnotized me on the spot.

"I lost outward consciousness. All of a sudden, an evil spirit came into my body and said, 'One of your best friends took that set of buttons at Shyam-bazar.* You will find it in a small box underneath a cot in the left-hand corner of his bedroom.'

"Mejda and Tulsi-da left immediately on their motorcycle for the friend's home, and found him there. The young man was shocked to see them, and seemed very nervous. Mejda went to his bedroom, found the box, and opened it. There were his buttons! His friend began crying. Mejda said to him, 'Do not enter my or Tulsi-da's home ever again.'

"They hurried back home, where I was still lying unconscious. Mejda thanked the evil spirit, then asked him to go. The spirit, however, liked it where he was, and replied, 'I will go only if you give me my

*A shopping place about two miles from their home.

22

freedom.' Mejda said, 'How can I do that? You are an evil spirit!'

"The spirit then said, 'If you don't, I won't leave. I'd rather kill her!' Master insisted, but the spirit simply wouldn't listen. Master then turned to Prakash Das and said, calmly but with deep intensity, 'Hand me the picture of Lahiri Mahasaya.' Holding that photograph, he said, 'Evil spirit, I will touch this body with the photograph in my hand if you don't leave.' The spirit cried out, 'All right! All right! I am going. But you must pray for my freedom.' Mejda agreed, and said that in time he would attain salvation. Then he blessed the spirit.

"As soon as the spirit was gone, Mejda began praying for me until I returned to consciousness. He then gave me some hot milk, and told me that my disposition was 'very soft.'* He blessed me, but it took another hour for me to feel well.

"Mejda never again used hypnosis for his own ends."

---

*He may have meant, "too susceptible."

Chapter Two

# A Trek in the Himalayas

In the month of June, one of Master's disciples, Dr. J. H. Clark, an SRF member and a medical doctor, came to Calcutta. He stayed at the YSS ashram in Baranagore. One day he asked Swamiji if he knew of anyone who could lead him on a tour of holy places in India. Swamiji knew that I'd traveled around the country and that I'd had some experience of hiking in the mountains, so he asked me to accompany our guest. I enthusiastically agreed.

A few days later, we set off on our tour that was to last thirty-five days. Our first stop was the city of Benares,* said to be the oldest still-inhabited city in the world. Anandamoyee Ma, the world-famous woman saint whom Yogananda describes reverently

---

*"Varanasi," as it is now called. This holiest city of the Hindus lies in the state of Uttar Pradesh, standing on the west bank of the River Ganges. For over 5,000 years pilgrims have come here. Holy to all Hindus, it is especially so to Shaivites, who worship God in the form of Shiva. Hindus deeply believe that all who die here achieve liberation. It was in Benares, so Paramhansa Yogananda said, that Babaji met Swami Shankaracharya many centuries ago, and initiated him into Kriya Yoga—a thrilling story, but, alas! not one for this book.

24

in *Autobiography of a Yogi,* had one of her ashrams there. My first meeting with her was at this ashram. I immediately understood why Master had described her as the "Joy-Permeated Mother." She and he had great soul-love for one another. She referred to him as "Baba," her common appellation for men, but one that seemed to have special meaning in his case.

We stayed there for four days, and were able to visit her twice a day. Each time she blessed us. I was captivated by her and by her transparent love for God. On many occasions she would go into *samadhi* (ecstasy) before us, sometimes for only half an hour, sometimes for hours at a time. In her divine love she was like a magnet. This, I felt, must have been what Master was like!

Anandamoyee Ma never stayed long at any of her ashrams, moving about to give more of her devotees a chance to be with her as much as possible. A strange fact I noted was that she never ate with her own hand. Her close women disciples would feed her, like a child.

As we were leaving, she asked us to return as often as we could. My heart was full to overflowing. After that first encounter I never let a year go by without visiting her at least once or twice. It wasn't long before she would know immediately when I had come, and would call out to me, "Come up here! Sit beside me." We were very close, and I treasure every moment that I was able to absorb myself in her vibrations.

One time she asked me to chant for her. I sang the

well-known *mahamantra,* or "great mantra," *Haré Krishna, haré Krishna, Krishna Krishna, haré, haré! Haré Ram, haré Ram, Ram Ram, haré, haré!* She loved to sing this chant with me, and thereafter often sang it with her disciples.

Whenever I recall those times, tears come to my eyes in loving gratitude for all that she taught me: surrender to the Infinite, non-attachment, inner peace, devotion to God and Guru. Her face, divinely beautiful, would be wreathed in smiles and surrounded by an aura of heavenly light and grace. She seemed to me not to belong to this world. At times, though looking directly at us, she was obviously far away, mentally. Although physically sitting before us, inwardly she was soaring to the heights of divine consciousness.

A devotee of Ma's has written, "The central theme of Her teaching, in endless variations, was: The supreme calling of every human being is to aspire to Self-realization. All other obligations are secondary. Only actions that kindle man's divine nature are worthy of the name of action. She often told us, 'In whatever circumstances you may find yourself placed, tell yourself: "It is all right; this is necessary for me. It is His way of drawing me to His feet, so let me be content." By Him alone should your heart be possessed. Your sorrow, your pain, your agony is indeed my own sorrow. This body [it was in this fashion that Ma referred to herself] understands everything.'"

As I wanted to know everything I could of her

saintly life, I once asked her, "When did you find God?"

She replied, "When I was six years old, and living with my father, mother, brother, and sister in my native village near Dacca [a city in what is now Bangladesh], we all went to the festivities in celebration of the goddess Durga [the festivities are called *Durgapuja*].* I was seated on the ground, watching people as they came forward to honor Durga. Suddenly I saw a moon forming upon the face of Durga's image. It approached me very slowly, then entered my heart. I lost outward consciousness for ten or fifteen minutes. It wasn't until my brother and sister got up to leave that, seeing me seated without motion, they shook me and said 'It's time to go home!' Only then did I come out of that trance. At that point I beheld the light leave me and return to the Durga *murti* (image)."

Hearing this story, I was thrilled in my heart. "Was that your first *samadhi?*" I asked Ma. She laughed and answered, "I do not know."

We left Benares the next morning for Delhi, and then Ranikhet, this time traveling by train. After a long 12-hour ride, we finally arrived at the secluded inn where we were to stay. It was owned by a very nice English lady, Mrs. Clark (not related to the man I was travelling with). She had been married to a

---

*Durgapuja* is one of the principal festivals in Bengal. Durga represents *shakti*, or energy, and is believed to help mankind to develop non-attachment to the material world.

British military major. After his death she bought this house, including many acres surrounding it, as a means of providing herself with a steady income. She loved it here in the lonely hill station of Ranikhet, overlooking as it did the snow-capped Himalaya mountains, despite the fact that the area was frequented by tigers and other wild animals. She had four large, woolly shepherd dogs to keep her company and also to protect her. She was able to serve many pilgrims on their travels to and from various ashrams and mountain retreats. This was the perfect spot for us, for Dr. Clark was a deep meditator, and sought solitude much of the time. The primitive aspects of the inn pleased him. As he said often to me, "No electricity: no harm!"

Dr. Clark was a simple person, and a very good devotee. His heart was always full of love. Many days we meditated together, and he would share with me spiritual blessings and insights he had received. He told me, "Master would say, 'Call God: He is always nearby'" As long as my body lives, I will never forget the blessings of our friendship, and will feel his love.

One afternoon Mrs. Clark invited us for tea. She addressed the doctor: "Being a Catholic, why do you follow an Indian Guru? Do you consider him above Christ?" Dr. Clark replied, "I do not see any barrier between my Guru and Jesus Christ. Rather, I have come to know who Christ was through Master." She then asked me if I believed in Christ. "Of course!" I said. "Jesus Christ had perfect Self-realization. I love him as I love my Guru."

From the inn we visited Babaji's cave, higher up near the Gogash River on Drona Giri mountain where, in 1861, Lahiri Mahasaya recognized his guru, Babaji, from former lives. It was here that Babaji initiated Lahiri Mahasaya into the sacred Kriya Yoga technique in a golden palace which, as we read in *Autobiography of a Yogi*, Babaji materialized for him. We also visited the ancient Drona Giri Temple, dedicated to Ma Kali,* and meditated there for hours. The mountain was named after *Dronacharya*, the famed teacher of the Pandavas and Kauravas in the *Mahabharata*. (This holy epic contains the best-loved scripture in India, the *Bhagavad Gita*.) It was here that Drona established his kingdom. How uplifting it was to be where Babaji once lived, and where Lahiri Mahasaya, meeting him again in this lifetime, received initiation into Kriya Yoga!

A beautiful saint, a *muni* or "silent sage," lived there also. We felt great blessings emanating from him as we sat in his presence. We also enjoyed our quiet time together during what proved to be a good four-hours' walk there from Mrs. Clark's.

The next day we left her inn for Delhi, from which point we proceeded to the hill town of Simla,

---

*Kali is a symbol of God in the aspect of eternal Mother Nature, and is an aspect of Durga. Master, as a child, worshiped Her, crying out to Her from his heart to reveal Herself—as, finally, She did with infinite sweetness and love. Kali was also the special object of adoration for Sri Ramakrishna.

where we remained for six days. Since Yoganandaji and Sri Yukteswar had made a pilgrimage here, Dr. Clark, desirous of following in their footsteps, wanted also to visit here. He also wanted to meditate in the *Hanuman Mandir* high on Jaku Hill.

Along the way to this temple, many monkeys (Hanuman is known as the "monkey god") came out and greeted us, chattering away. They were well-behaved monkeys, however! Dr. Clark had bought bananas, sweets, and nuts for them, and as we entered the area the monkeys stretched out their hands for their treat. Fortunately, we were well provided!

Soon we returned to Calcutta* for a week to visit Master's boyhood home at 4 Garpar Road, and my own home as well. We had a meal with Tulsi Bose and his family, and with Atmanandaji. Afterwards we visited the Kali Temple in Dakshineswar, and two other temples: Belur Math, founded by Swami Vivekananda (chief disciple of Ramakrishna), and the Tarakeshwar Shiva Temple, at which, as in Lourdes, France, many people have been miraculously healed of their illnesses: physical, emotional, mental, and spiritual.

After a week in Calcutta, Dr. Clark returned to America. His visit had been a blessing for us all, but especially for me, who had been able to spend so much time with him alone.

---

*At that time, Calcutta was not devastated as it now is by pollution, over-crowding, and unbelievable numbers of automobiles. It was, in general, a wonderful city, and provided a good life for its inhabitants.

## Chapter Three

# A Visit from Mt. Washington

A few weeks after that, Sister Sailasuta, a direct disciple of Yogananda's from the SRF Mt. Washington monastery, came to Calcutta. She showed deep reverence for her guru, and radiated to everyone great joy and energy from a heart that was warm and expansive. We soon became good friends.

Sister Sailasuta with me and Hassi

Master gave her the nickname of Sailasuta, meaning "daughter of the mountains," because she was a good hiker. Oh, how she loved to recall how Master had called her that! (After his passing, she took Sailasuta as her monastic name because of the fondness of those memories.) She was a fast hiker, and whenever we climbed a hill together she was always "up there" while I was still "down here"!

One day she asked me to accompany her to Puri, where Sri Yukteswar had had a seaside ashram. The ashram was now owned by YSS.

We were privileged, in Puri, to be able to visit Sri Bhupen Sanyal Mahasaya, a direct disciple of Lahiri Mahasaya, and to meditate in his presence every evening. He used to say, "Don't gossip: Just meditate!" At our request, he would often relate the teachings of Lahiri Mahasaya, his *gurudeva,* or tell us stories about him. With great enthusiasm he spoke of things he had heard directly from Lahiri's wife, Kashi Moni.

"One day," he said, "a few disciples had gathered at Guruji's home. Some of them had expressed a desire for the higher Kriya Yoga initiations. Guruji looked at them, smiling. Just then, the front door opened. In came the postman, Brinda Bhagat. Lahiri greeted him: 'Ah, Brinda! Would you like to receive the second Kriya initiation?'

"'Oh, please, Master, no!' Brinda protested. 'What would I do with higher initiations? I came here to ask a favor: I am so filled with God's presence already that I am hardly able to deliver my mail. Please, Guruji, would you request the Divine Postmaster to release me from my work, so that I can devote more time to the initiation I have received already?' Those impatient devotees were shamed to silence!"

I was told on a number of occasions that Lahiri Mahasaya used to bestow the higher Kriya initiations according to what the people themselves actually needed—that is to say, according to what would truly be effective for them, and not just for the sake of "getting more," greedily. Some of his disciples never received more than one initiation, even though they were with him for many years. Lahiri Mahasaya would say to them, "One is enough for you." Others, such as Sanyal Mahasaya, received three initiations. I know of four that Sri Yukteswar received.

On another occasion Sanyal Mahasaya told us, "One of Lahiri Mahasaya's close disciples and her husband wanted to come to Guruji's home for a puja ceremony. They were late in getting to the train station, however, and arrived just as the train was pulling out. Anxiously they prayed to our guru for help. Suddenly, the train stopped! The engineer stepped down. The stationmaster ran out. General concern! What could the trouble be? Meanwhile, the couple boarded the train. The puzzled engineer got back on and tried once again to get the train moving. This time it started out of the station as if nothing had happened! The couple could not doubt that this was a miracle caused by Guruji's intervention.

"The following morning, when they reached Lahiri Mahasaya's home, he scolded them with a smile saying, 'Next time, be on time! I had to call on God's power to get you on that train.'"

Another time Sanyal told us, "One morning Lahiri Mahasaya's wife Kashi Moni ('Guru Ma,' as we liked to call her) rushed into the Master's room to scold him about the household finances—or, rather, the lack of them. She spoke loudly, but didn't find him there. Thinking he must have gone outside, she raised her voice even louder. Suddenly she beheld her husband—who was her guru, also—seated in the lotus pose near the ceiling, suspended in air!

"'It is all nothing, don't you see?' he said to her. 'How could a nothing like me provide support for your earthly needs?' Beside herself with terror, she implored his forgiveness. Quietly, then, she slipped out of the room. Never again did she think of him as her husband. He was only her divine guru! Kashi Moni learned to see Lord Shiva, Destroyer of delusion, in the form of her husband. Soon afterward, a disciple of his offered material support for the family."

Sanyal Mahasaya said that his guru often told his disciples, "'*Bon-e, kon-e, mon-e!*' That is to say, 'Whether in a forest, in your room at home, or only in your own mind, be always with God.'"

We visited Sanyal Mahasaya several times more. Every time he blessed us, we felt the presence of the Divine. He would often quote Lahiri Mahasaya's advice, "If you don't invite God to be your summer guest, he won't come to you in the winter of your life." Throughout my life I have remembered the inspiration I drew from Sanyal Mahasaya.

It was in 1962 that Bhupendra Sanyal left his body.

\* \* \* \* \*

After a few days in Puri, we left to visit Ranchi, the town where Yogananda's school first became firmly established. It was here also that Master had his vision telling him to go to America, and showing him many future disciples in that country. I couldn't help thinking that Sailasuta was one of those disciples!

Anandamoyee Ma had an ashram also in Ranchi, where we visited every afternoon for *satsang,* and to receive her blessing. Many times we sat before her in meditation, not speaking for long periods. She went often into *samadhi,* or chanted softly. We went only with the purpose of being in her holy vibrations.

Four days later we returned to Calcutta and the Dakshineswar ashram. One day after our arrival, Swami Atmanandaji asked me please to build a retaining wall to prevent the bank of mud at one of the ashram boundary lines from slipping into the river. For three months I was prevented, therefore, from visiting saints in the Himalayan foothills. I'd become accustomed to trekking there, roaming about as I pleased and meeting advanced souls in secluded caves or huts. But I was grateful also to be in my guru's ashram, and passed the summer months there happily.

Finally the wall (and also a guest room) was finished. I was free at last, then, to return to my beloved mountains.

This time I went to Ranikhet and stayed once again at Mrs. Clark's hotel. A well-known fortune teller, named Rani Ma, lived nearby. At some point I befriended her. It didn't take me long, however, to realize that fortune telling was not a worthy occupation for her. I asked her, "Why do you spend so much of your time in this way? Why not teach the people who come here with shallow questions the path of meditation? In that way, they might get their own answers. That, surely, would be much more helpful to them." Rani Ma was a sincere devotee of Lord Rama. I could see she had much deeper things to give people.

One evening around 9 p.m., as I was walking slowly back from visiting Rani Ma, my thoughts on the conversation earlier that evening, I heard a noise and looked up. A large tigress was on a rock above the road, crouched as if ready to leap down on me! Her gaze was focused intently on my face! I loudly chanted, "Jai Ram! Jai Ram! Jai Guru!"

The tigress turned away and jumped down towards the valley below. I don't pretend to know for certain why she didn't attack me, but I have always believed it was by the grace of my great guru. Needless to say, I was overwhelmed with gratitude.

A few days later, this same tigress—an obviously

persistent beast!—returned and entered the grounds surrounding Mrs. Clark's hotel. The tigress was just about to attack one of the dogs that always guarded the inn, when all *four* dogs charged her. They clawed at her face ferociously, and tore out her eyes. Eventually they succeeded in killing her. One of the dogs was seriously wounded, and I had to call the local police. There was no recourse, unfortunately, but to shoot her.

My heart pounded for a long time after this episode. Among my other emotions, the reflection came that I never would have believed that dogs could kill a tiger! The ways of Nature are often strange. Every creature has a certain destiny—determined among lower animals, so Master wrote, by "group karma." I certainly felt part, that day, of the magnificence of cosmic Mother Nature!

Soon thereafter I met a very advanced soul, Kailash Pati, who lived on Kalika Hill about four miles from Ranikhet. Pilgrims sometimes ask the sadhus they meet to tell them their fortunes. If a sadhu of deep intuition sees something that may be helpful for a person to know, he may speak. Otherwise, he will remain silent. I myself do not believe in asking for such things. I travel in the mountains only to be with great souls who spend their lives in God, or in seeking Him. I therefore never asked Kailash Pati for any favor. He was very happy to see that I'd come for purely spiritual reasons. Over the six years that I got to visit him, I had a chance to meditate with him for long periods of time. Each of those meditations holds precious memories for me. I would sit with him while he remained in *samadhi* for hours at a time.

Before I left the first time, he encouraged me to visit a great yogi, Hari Gauri, in the small nearby town of Naini Tal, giving me directions to the saint's home. He hinted that the trip would not be easy, but it didn't dawn on me that the way there would prove dangerous. It wasn't until the summer of 1958 that I finally got my chance to go see him. Much of the trail was, in fact, so narrow that in many places it was only *one-and-a-half-feet-wide!*

On the outskirts of Naini Tal there is a large, serene lake. A mandir, or sacred temple, stands majestically at the north end of the lake. I stayed at a small inn for the night. The next morning I left for the Hari Gauri Mandir, though in fact I was seeking the living Hari Gauri.

Someone local to the area told me I would find it three and a half kilometers behind the Governor's forest bungalow. I went first to the temple and bowed to Naini Devi, the *murti* of Divine Mother that is worshiped there. Then I began to walk in search of Hari Gauri. From the directions I'd been given, I knew that after several kilometers I would see a large tree, from which point I must turn left and climb a hill toward the ashram.

As I was walking I talked mentally to my Divine Mother Kali, singing Her praises. In doing so, however, I was paying insufficient attention to my surroundings, and missed the large tree. More than a mile farther on, I realized that I was lost. I stopped in confusion. Just then a young girl, typical of the hill people, came towards me with a bundle of wood in her arms. It surprised me to see a hill girl alone in that deep jungle. Usually, people traveling there would go in groups of fifteen or more for protection.

"Where are you going?" she asked me. "Are you lost?" She spoke in the accent of hill people: similar to Hindi, but slightly different also. She added, "Don't go any further. There are tigers living beyond this spot. Come, follow me."

I asked her why she was walking alone so deep in the forest, but she only smiled and repeated, "Follow me."

After about fifteen minutes we came to the tall, stately tree I had been told to look out for. Here she said, "Go up this path here. It's just a few minutes farther." I turned from glancing at the path to thank her. To my amazement, she was no longer there! I shouted loudly. Still, I heard no response.

My body perspired and my eyes filled with tears, for I realized just Who this little girl had been. Fervently I thanked my Divine Mother Kali. After waiting a few minutes, hoping to catch a glimpse of Her, I proceeded on my way.

Hari Gauri was waiting for me before the gate. "Welcome, welcome!" he said. "Divine Mother saved you. Next time, watch where you are going! Follow Kailash Pati's instructions."

In his mandir I found a beautiful statue of Kali. We meditated before it for four hours. The whole time I chanted, "Kali, Kali!" I could not check my tears. Afterwards, this saintly man invited me in to eat *kitchuri* (a simple dish of rice, daal, and vegetables) with him.

As we were eating, Hari Gauri told me he had met Paramhansa Yogananda while he lived in the United States for four years working as an electrical engineer. He had great love and regard for Master. After a while, I said it was time for me to leave as I didn't want to impose on his time any longer. However, he asked me first to come into his small hut. It had a room containing two beds, and another room for meditation and *asana*s (yoga postures). The place had very powerful vibrations. Inside was a woman, whom he introduced to me as Gauri.

"Do you know who she is?" he asked. I told him I thought she must be his partner in *tantra*. "She is that also," he replied, "but she is far more. She is my mother, my sister, my friend, and last of all my legitimate wife." Both of them said, "May Divine Mother Kali bless you."

The next day I left for Benares to spend three days with Anandamoyee Ma, after that returning once more to Dakshineswar.

## Chapter Four

# An Official Visit from SRF

Upon my arrival back, in 1958, Atmanandaji informed me that in mid-October Daya Mata, the president of Self-Realization Fellowship, would be coming with a group of monastics from the Self-Realization Fellowship headquarters in Los Angeles, California. This would be SRF's first official visit to YSS.

We monks worked very hard from then on to get everything ready for their arrival. Soon, everything was "spic and span."

Daya Mata and her sister Mataji (who later took the name Ananda Mata, and was also a board member), Swami Kriyananda, and Sister Revati, arrived at Calcutta's Dum Dum airport at noon on the appointed day, in a driving monsoon rain. A large contingent—some fifty of us—were on hand to greet them with garlands to symbolize our love. Their luggage was collected, and we drove to the Baranagore ashram.

At this time I was living in the Dakshineswar

*math,* or monastery. Atmanandaji, however, asked me to come every day to Baranagore and look after our visitors. Dayama was most kind to me. She exclaimed, "You come all the way from Dakshineswar every day on foot?" Quietly she gave me money to buy a bicycle so as to make the journey easier.

Many evenings she would come to the math in Dakshineswar also, for meditation. Some evenings, while gliding along the Ganges in a large rented rowboat, she told me stories about Master and of how he had affected the lives of all those around him.

In the early years, she said on one of those evenings, Master was faced with great financial difficulties. No money was available to pay the bills or the mortgage, or even to give the devotees enough to live on. He was deeply concerned. Was Divine Mother pleased with the work he was doing for Her? "Mother," he prayed, "I never wanted all this! I've done it only to please You. If You are not satisfied, I will gladly return to India." For many months he received no answer to this prayer.

Finally She appeared to him! In a glorious vision She said, "I am your stocks and bonds. What more dost thou need than that thou hast Me? Dance of life and dance of death: Know that these come from Me, and as such, rejoice!" Very soon after that, Master's financial problems were ended by a wealthy and very dear disciple.

Dayama also shared with me how he had wanted to return to India for the last years of his life, to look after the work in India. In the end, however, he never got the "go ahead" from Divine Mother, who withheld Her blessings from this cherished project.

Daya Mata was very happy to know that, through my supervision, all the work had been completed on the guest house and the retaining wall at Dakshineswar. She also thanked Tulsi Bose for his part in purchasing the land. Master had written to Prakash Das, by then a director of YSS, to name the Calcutta ashram, "Tulsi-Yogoda Ashram." In fact, he wanted Yogoda Math and the other ashrams also to have this name. Because the name of the Society was Yogoda Sat-Sanga Society, however, and because Yogoda Math was the main headquarters of YSS at that time, the name elsewhere, with Master's approval, remained unchanged.

*Yogoda* was a name created by Paramhansa Yogananda. It was intended as a contraction of two words: *yoga,* and *da,* "da" in this case meaning "that which gives." A society, in other words, that teaches, or "gives," yoga. Binay Dubey, a late visitor to the work (it was only considerably later that he became a member),* objected to this name.

"Yoga," he said, "is spelled with an *a*. It is not 'yogo.'" Then he was reminded that he himself, when speaking Bengali, pronounced yoga with the

---

*Eventually he was appointed by Daya Mata to its top administrative position.

Bengali accent, *"jogaw."* Finally Dubey agreed that "yogoda" might be considered a legitimate coinage. It would have been highly inconvenient, certainly, to change the name after all these years!

I mention this incident to say that from this time onward a new spirit began entering YSS. Binayendra Nath Dubey was not at this time even a member. Yet he never hesitated to tell Daya Ma things that, he insisted, the people in America, and all of us in India, and even a great Indian master (Yogananda) ought (according to him) to have known. His presumption of our ignorance was extraordinary.

Quelled on his objection to the name, "Yogoda," he then proceeded to point out that the organization, which at that time bore the name, "Yogoda Sat-Sanga Society" with "Sat-Sanga" hyphenated, ought not to be abbreviated "YSS," but rather to have a third "s": in other words, "YSSS." This seemed a trivial point to us, a mere technicality hardly worth even considering. Dubey, however, made an issue of it, and despite everyone's lack of interest kept on insisting. The obvious was pointed out to him: that "YSSS" was awkward to pronounce. No matter. We learned in time that Dubey's nature was to persist, even in minor matters, until he'd got his way. At last, a compromise was agreed upon: Sat-Sanga was combined into one word. Thus, the official name became Yogoda Satsanga Society, and the abbreviation, as before, YSS.

One could not but wonder at this fuss over such a small issue. In time, however, it became clear that by this little opening he had gained entry into the "inner sanctum" of organizational power, and areas that normally would be open only to inside, long-term members.

Dubey's intrusion was not so much noticed by Dayama, who was herself new to the Indian scene, as it was by us Indians, who had been serving Master's work in this country for many years. His presumption—for so we could only consider it—though relatively minor at first, continued unabated. Though he was still not a member, and not even a devotee of this path, he made increasingly bold rec-ommendations even to the point of declaring force-fully (as one who, being himself Indian, was "in the know" on such things) who ought to give Kriya ini-tiation; how Kriya should be given; what a teacher's role needed to be in the organization, and other quite fundamental matters. He urged that *all* power be centralized in the person of the SRF/YSS presi-dent, even to her having the sole right to give Kriya initiation. (Others, he said, should be permitted to give Kriya only as her representatives). He urged the supreme spiritual importance of the president, even as the "living guru" of all who took Kriya initiation. Other matters also he stressed on subjects quite cen-tral to the organization, and not at all in keeping with the pattern Master himself had established. Dubey insisted that his ideas *must* have been Master's wish also, as this was how these things were done in India. He even insisted that Master, when he wore Western clothes in the streets of Los

Angeles, must at least have kept an orange handkerchief in his pocket—"Otherwise," he declared, waving a finger affirmatively, "he was *no* swami!"

Dubey managed ultimately so far to influence the direction of YSS's, and ultimately SRF's, growth that some of the customs most clearly established by Master were drastically changed. How, we all wondered, could one man have gained so much influence in a spiritual organization to which he was a veritable newcomer? It was not as though he had committed himself to the organization, or even to the yogic life. He was, in fact, what one might call a spiritual drifter.

Well, more of this important issue later.

To resume my story: One day we drove into Calcutta to visit Master's family home at 4 Garpar Road. It was from here that Master had left for America to begin his world-wide mission. And it was here also, in his small "attic room," where, as he put it, "I found God." His younger brother Sananda Lal lived there now, with his wife Parul, and their son and daughter Hare Krishna and Shefali. We meditated in the attic room, and heard from them many stories of our guru's life.

From there we continued on to Tulsi Bose's home, where Master stayed after his return to India in 1935. Here, in the family meditation room, Master had meditated countless times. Sri Yukteswar, Master's gurudeva, had also blessed this spot; also Anandamoyee Ma and other great souls. At Tulsida's home we met others of Master's disciples. The

SRF representatives were filled with love for this "grand family."

Tulsi was reserved by nature, speaking little. His ways were simple: a strictly vegetarian diet, and no cigarettes or alcohol. Out of deep respect for Master, born of an understanding of who Master was, Tulsi-da always did whatever Master asked him to do. The two of them were deeply devoted to one another throughout their lives.

Tulsi told Daya Mata and the others many incidents of Master's early life, and spoke glowingly of what Master had always meant to him. He invited the Americans to stay for dinner, which Martan Ma and Dakha (their cook) had prepared for them. Dakha had joined the family even before their daughter, Hassi, was born. She had also cooked for Sri Yukteswar, for Richard Wright (Dayama's brother, who accompanied Master to India in 1935), and for many other devotees.

"One touching event occurred one morning during the winter months," Tulsi-da told them, "Yogananda came downstairs and saw Martan Ma shivering a little from the cold. He took the shawl from around his shoulders and placed it lovingly around hers, saying, 'Now, Mother, you won't be cold any longer.' Oh, how great was his affection for her!" That shawl now resides, beautifully displayed, in the Shrine of the Masters museum at Ananda Village in California.

## Chapter Five

# Tulsi Bose, Yogananda's Boyhood Friend

Tulsi-da once told me how he had come to know Master. "One afternoon," he said, "in May, 1909, I was resting on a bench in Greer Park, near my home. I had just completed an invigorating run, and was thinking about the big hockey match that was scheduled the next day. All of a sudden, I saw this long-haired boy come up to me. I didn't recognize him, and was certain we had never met before. He asked, 'Aren't you Tulsi Bose?'

"Astonished, I replied, 'But who are *you?*'

"Again he said, 'First, tell me: Are you Tulsi Bose?' 'Yes,' I replied, 'I am.' He sat down beside me on the bench. Then he asked me, 'Aren't you a hockey player and a runner?'

"By this time I was surprised not only by this boy's abruptness, but by his persistent interest in me. I had just barely got out a halting 'Yes . . .' when, sure of me now, he cut in quickly, 'All right, let's run together!' I didn't see why we shouldn't, so we started out at a fast clip.

"For the first lap we were running side by side. By the end of the second lap, however, he was ten feet ahead of me. I couldn't believe my eyes! I was a very good runner, and besides, I knew all the runners in our vicinity. Who was this boy? Where did he come from?

"I was breathing quite heavily from my efforts to beat this upstart! Yet how could I quit? I didn't want to be defeated! So I said, 'Let's do it a second time.' This time, I ran as fast as I could. Still, I couldn't beat him.

"Finally I asked him, 'How is it you can run so fast? Your stride is not that of a runner at all.' He replied, 'I will teach you. Come to my home tonight.'

"'But where is your home?' I said. 'Number 4 Garpar Road,' he replied.

"'Why, that is the home of Bhagabati Babu!'

"'Yes,' he replied. 'I am his son Mukunda. Tonight I will tell you also how I found you, and why. From now on,' he added, 'I will call you Tulsi-da.'

"At midnight I reached Mukunda's home at 4 Garpar Road. He was standing outside waiting for me. We entered the house together and went to his room on the ground floor. He shut the door, and we sat down, arranging our legs in the lotus pose. He then touched my forehead, and my mind became completely still. He taught me some yoga meditation techniques, and we remained there the whole night.

Before leaving the house early the next morning I got to hear the story of how and why he had found me.

"'It has not been quiet here at home,' Mukunda said, 'with so many children running all over the place, and guests always coming. I've found it disturbing not to have time for solitude and meditation. One day I cried to Divine Mother Kali, "Please give me one good, devoted friend with a quiet home where I can be more with You." Later, I was walking down the street near our house when suddenly I

Left: The painting of Krishna by Hari Narayan Bose, father of Tulsi Bose

Right: Atmananda in later years. The original painting of Krishna is on the wall behind him.

50

went into a trance. In vision I saw a young man about my own age playing in front of what seemed to be his family home. Divine Mother said to me, "That boy is a good devotee, and loves Me very much. You will get all the help you want from him and his family." Hearing these words, my eyes filled with tears. Mentally I bowed at Her feet, thanking Her for Her love for me. It was soon after that we met.'

"I invited Mukunda to our house the next evening for dinner. He came over in the afternoon and I introduced him to my father, Hari Narayan Bose. Father was very happy on seeing him, and told him, 'It feels as though you were a part of our family already! What is time when recognition is so sudden?' "Mukunda did become an honorary member of our family. He used to address my father as *Baba Mahasaya* ('Father with a great soul'). Ever since that afternoon in the park, we two boys spent much of our time together."

The following year, Mukunda's cousin Prabhas-da joined the two friends. Together they would go to Dakshineswar and sit under the *Panchavati,* or *Bel* tree, on the temple grounds, for night meditations.

Tulsi continued, "One day, in 1919, I was talking with Mukunda about the advanced yogic state called *samadhi.* He said to me, 'Come sit here beside me. Practice the Kriya I have taught you.' I did so. He then touched my forehead. Suddenly I lost outer consciousness. My awareness began spiraling

51

upwards. I saw countless radiant beings, beautiful scenes—other worlds!

"'How was it?' he asked. I told him what I had seen and how beautiful it all was. 'Please,' I said, 'show me how I can be in that state all the time.' He laughed and replied, 'These experiences are not for you in this lifetime. You must wait till your next life. Meanwhile, do Kriya every day, and live a very simple existence.'

"One day," Tulsi continued, "my father, concerned for my future, asked Mukunda if I would go to the Himalayas and live out my life as a yogi. Mukunda answered him, 'Tulsi-da will not go there. He will stay here with you, marry, and have three daughters, one of whom however will not live long.' Everything came to pass as he'd said. I married, had three daughters, and one of them died when she was only four years old. The other two lived."

I must add here, parenthetically, that the youngest daughter, Hassi, years later became my wife.

Tulsi's account continues:

"Two years later, when my father heard that Mukunda wanted a place in which to hold meditation classes, he purchased the plot of land behind our home and gave it to us boys, along with the money to build a three-room thatched hut where we could have our meditations and be alone with God. It was in this way that Mukunda began his very first school."

Swami Kebalanandaji, a deep yogi and noted Sanskrit scholar, soon began teaching there. He was a devotee of Lahiri Mahasaya, who called him *Shastri Mahasaya,* which is to say, "Learned in the soul-meaning of the scriptures." Mukunda was thrilled to have such a divine mentor. Together they spent many hours daily, learning the teachings of the great ones.

Friends who were sincere in their search for God often joined Mukunda and Tulsi-da in their new school. In 1916 a devotee offered Mukunda a piece of land in Dihika that could serve as a better place for a rapidly growing school. Then it was, also, that Mukunda took his monastic vows from his guru Sri Yukteswar, becoming known from then on as Swami Yogananda.

Sri Yukteswarji came to Tulsi's home to see Yogananda's school ashram before they moved to Dihika. It wasn't long, however, before they had to leave Dihika also, owing to an outbreak of malaria. In this dilemma, the Maharaja of Kashimbazar came to the rescue. He offered Swami Yogananda a plot of land in Ranchi, Bihar. To those grounds, in 1918, Yogananda eventually moved his school. In this salubrious climate, a growing body of students came in order to learn "the ways of God and mathematics." Two years passed. Then Divine Mother called Yogananda to America.

Tulsi-da, in speaking to Daya Mata and the others of her group, recalled fondly, "He never forgot me. He would write often from America and tell me and my family of his experiences in that new land. It was hard to imagine what his life was really like. I wondered if I would ever see him again.

"Then, in 1926, my father passed away. In 1927 I married Martan Ma. Guruji had picked her out for me, and blessed her and also our first daughter."

Later, when Master returned to India in 1935, he stayed with Tulsi and Martan Ma in their home. He also blessed their third child in Martan's womb, saying, "This child will be a girl, and will be very devoted." He gave Martan an apple "for the baby," whose name was Hassi, which means, "Laughter." Indeed, Hassi has always been blessed with a happy disposition.

Tulsi and Master traveled together to many places. One day they were meditating together with Prakash Das and Jitendra (Jiten) Mazumdar,* when one of Tulsi's cousins rushed into the room crying urgently, "Come quickly! It's my wife; she's dying!"

The two doctors in attendance had told him there was no hope for her recovery. The cousin knew Master, however, and had deep faith in him. Therefore, "hoping against hope," he had come here for help. Master told the others to come along.

On arriving at the cousin's home, Master went immediately into the bedroom. There, asking the others to wait outside, he closed the door. Meanwhile, another highly respected physician came to see what he could do. He too was obliged to wait

*Who accompanied Mukunda on the famous episode, "Two Penniless Boys in Brindaban," from *Autobiography of a Yogi.*

outside. More than forty-five minutes passed. Finally, Master came out of the room; the cousin's wife came with him, walking without assistance! The doctors, all three of whom were there, were astounded. This, they exclaimed, was truly a miracle.

Master said to the husband, "After we leave, she will sleep one or two days. Don't be alarmed, and don't call her. She will be all right, and will eventually regain her full strength."

Not a word passed between the friends after they left. They were overcome by what they'd witnessed. On arriving at Tulsi's home, Master asked Dakha to cook him a curry. Rajaram, a young man who served as the housekeeper, later gave him a massage to help restore the energy he'd given out.

After that, the cousin's wife came frequently to see Master, and eventually took initiation and discipleship from him.

"One day," Tulsi-da said, "Guruji took us to *Shantiniketan* ('Abode of Peace') to visit the great poet Rabindranath Tagore. Guruji told us he was a highly advanced soul. After we'd been there awhile, and were preparing to start back to Calcutta, Master asked Tagore, 'How do you feel (meaning, about his life)?' The poet replied spontaneously in poetic style:

> Yes, I am a Traveler.
> Nothing can hold me back.
> Pleasure and pain seek to bind me,
> But, ah! my home lies far beyond.

His non-attachment impressed me deeply.

Tulsi understood Tagore's desire to be released from banal office work, for he too had never held a traditional job. Indeed, he had never held any job at all! He spent all his time doing *sadhana,* as Master had asked him to do.

It was about this time that Master announced a wish to purchase a large piece of land on the bank of the Ganges. Prakash Das began the search for the perfect ashram setting. At last they found, in Dakshineswar, a three-and-a-half-acre piece right on the Ganges. Master went twice to see it, and finally decided to buy it. He sent Prakash Das to fix the price, telling him, "As soon as I return to America, I will send you the money for the final purchase."

Master left India at the end of 1936. Prakash Das sent him a hundred photographs of the land, from different perspectives. The property was finally purchased in 1939. Master was very happy. It became a place of great peace—ideal for meditation!

## Chapter Six

# Ranchi—Then, a Trek to Badrinath!

After the Americans had been with us about two weeks, Dayama said one morning, "Would you like to go with us to Ranchi today?" I said, "Of course!" I joined our SRF guests. Binay Dubey came along also. Paramananda had purchased a big Studebaker car in which we'd already traveled to many places that Dayama had wanted to see. In Ranchi we stayed at "Wood House," which Paramananda's father, J.B. Wood, had built. Mr. Wood was a disciple of Master who often came to India from his home in Florida to stay for months at a time—residing mostly, however, at the Baranagore ashram.

One day we had a soccer game. Kriyananda captained the teachers; I captained the students. I hadn't realized that Kriyananda was so good at soccer! We all enjoyed the game very much. Afterwards, Dayama gave us all candy and encouraged us to play often.

We returned to Calcutta after twelve days. Then

the SRF group went on to Delhi and Kashmir. Dubey
went with them again.

In time I developed a good friendship with
Kriyanandaji. Among other things, he spoke much
about Master. One day he surprised me by saying
that Master had taught him to make samosas (which
he called *singharas*, Bengali fashion) and other
Indian foods. This impressed me very much! Sometimes also he scolded me gently for spending so
much time in the mountains. "Why don't you stay
here with us more?" he asked, teasingly. "We need
your help." But my heart longed for the Himalayas.
Besides, he knew that I worked very hard every time
I came back, and expressed appreciation for this
service. But he was concerned for YSS, which he per-
ceived as barely bumping along, when there was so
much to do here for Master's work.

In April of 1959, I set out for a Himalayan tour,
leaving from Rishikesh* on foot with two monks
from the Sivananda† ashram. The trip we planned
was 450 miles, round-trip. It took us many weeks to

---

*Rishikesh, or "City of Sages," contains many ashrams along
the Ganges River banks in a beautiful rural setting in the
foothills of the great Himalayas. Located near the point where
the mighty river emerges from the mountains, it is the spot from
which pilgrims leave for the high country. Several miles below it
is Haridwar, or Hardwar, "Doorway to the Himalayas": land of
Hari (Krishna) or Hara (Shiva), depending on whom you worship. The Himalayas generally are thought of as the "abode of
Shiva."

†Swami Sivananda was a master yogi and the founder and head
of the world-known Divine Life Society, which has monks and
representatives in many lands, sharing the ancient yoga teachings.

complete. Meanwhile, Kriyanandaji, infected by some of my "wanderlust," made a trip on his own to Kashmir. Not, however, on foot!

In India it is considered extremely auspicious, and is every devotee's lifelong dream, to make a pilgrimage to the Himalayas. Centuries ago, when the world was shrouded in spiritual darkness and ignorance, the great master Swami Shankara injected new life into India by promoting religious and national unity. In pursuit of that mission, he established four *jyotirmath*s, or education centers for monks, to diffuse divine light throughout the land. He established these *math*s in the four corners of India. These centers still exist, and are located in Mysore (in the south), Puri (in the east), Dwarka (in the west), and Badrinath (in the north, high above Rishikesh). All of these places have deep spiritual significance and power, and have been honored by Hindus for millennia.

In the Himalayas there are also four sacred spots connected with Badrinath and making a holy pilgrimage loop: Badrinath of course, then Kedarnath, Yamunotri, and Gangotri. We hoped to complete the entire loop safely with the blessings of our gurus and of the saints we'd meet along the way.

The first day we left very early in the morning, heading for Gangotri. We left with light hearts, our minds and hearts focused on what we fully expected would be an extraordinary adventure. What lay ahead of us? Would we even be able to complete our long journey?

Soon, along the way, we met a few swamis living in caves deep in the forest. Reaching Gangotri, we could see the impressive *Gomukh*, the beginning of the Ganges, where "Ganga" (the Indian name for the River Ganges) emerges through what is thought to resemble the mouth of a cow (*Go:* "cow"; in ancient Sanskrit, as the sage Sri Aurobindo discovered, it also means "light"; and *mukh:* "mouth"). Here Ganga emerges as a beautiful waterfall created by a melting glacier. From this point she begins her downward journey to the plains. Gomukh emerges from the foot of the impressive Shivling Peak (6543m), whose snow-laden slopes shimmered high above us in the glare of the summer sun, brilliant against the deep blue sky. Nineteen kilometers beyond Gomukh lies Gangotri at a height of 3140m.

As we approached Gangotri, the country opened out before us into a valley surrounded by jagged, snow-covered peaks. The slopes were covered by birch trees, their trunks wrapped in bark which looked like paper tissue. This material was used in ancient times for recording the scriptures, after the science of writing became not so much a discovery as a necessity owing to the increasing shortness of human memory. The mountain slopes also contain groups of giant boulders; they seem to stand guard as huge sentinels in a valley of the gods.

The river flows north here, giving the village its name Gangotri: "Ganga turned north." One misstep on this path, and a person would fall 5,000 feet!

Walking 8–10 hours a day, we eventually came to

*Triyugnarayan,* an ancient Narayan Krishna temple. Here we stopped for the night to visit Muni Baba, a highly advanced soul who hadn't spoken for fifty years. As we greeted him, he indicated with hand gestures that he would be happy for us to meditate with him. Later on, he blessed us. No one could tell what he ate. When I asked him, he simply raised his hands to heaven as if to say, "By God's grace." There was a depth of stillness around him, a sure sign of a God-realized soul.

The following day we left for Rudra Prayag, famous now for the exploits of Jim Corbett, the English hunter who saved hundreds of villagers from the predations of a large feline that he later described in a book named, *The Man-Eating Leopard of Rudra Prayag.* He also slew many man-eating tigers in the Himalayas, especially in the *Kumaon* hills\* in the Almora district. One of these tigers had killed over 125 people. Corbett and others had noticed that the tiger was not killing the goats, cows, and other animals that are its usual food, but only human beings. The villagers pleaded with Jim to hunt it down and destroy it. So, in order to create a lure for the beast, he built a three-sided bungalow with no roof, and asked a few men to go inside the structure and wait for the tiger to come. I imagine a certain decrease in their enthusiasm at this point! He assured them, however, "Don't be afraid. I will be here, and will

\*Swami Kriyananda used to take seclusion in this area.

61

protect you from harm." He then climbed up a tall mango tree above the pretense bungalow, and waited.

Toward midnight the tiger could be heard approaching. Jim Corbett, seeing it, intentionally made a noise. The tiger glanced up at him, making itself an easy target. Jim instantly shot it dead.

Corbett's adventures with these deadly animals resulted in the local residents revering him as a kind of savior. That mango tree is now famous.

At 11 p.m. we arrived at the small town, and saw lights in the room where people were staying overnight. Surprised, then alarmed, we saw police all over the area, carrying guns. They told us not to move, not knowing who or what we were. They told us they'd just caught seven persons with matted hair and beards in the very room where we had been planning to stay. These men were not sadhus at all, but only pretended to be so. In fact, they were *dacoits*: cutthroats and robbers. The police asked us to accompany them, along with the dacoits, up to the police station. The superintendent of police took the dacoits outside and proceeded to beat them severely with bamboo sticks. We were stunned and horrified, though helpless to do anything but pray for the miscreants. These men were, after all, only fellow human beings caught in one of the many webs of delusion.

The superintendent then called us into a room to interrogate us. I showed him our letters of invitation, our vaccination certificates, and a letter from

YSS. He was satisfied on seeing these documents, and said, "I can see that there are no dacoits in this group!" They then offered us tea and samosas. The superintendent asked one policeman to help us find our rooms, and reassured us that we would be guarded all night. No more incidents occurred, and we left the next morning for Kedarnath.

Now we had to cross *Guptakashi*. It was here, in surroundings rich with colorful and incredibly beautiful landscapes, that Shiva is said to have come to hide from the Pandavas, who were seeking him out to ask redemption for any sins they may have committed during the great war of the *Mahabharata*. To escape detection, the Lord lived incognito. The town here, therefore, is called Gupta (hidden) Kashi.

From this spot we proceeded to Gauri Kund, where Parvati is said to have meditated for hundreds of years to win Lord Shiva as her consort. Water from this *kund* (hot springs) falls into the Mandakini River, which flows nearby. From here, the temple of Kedarnath is distant about seven kilometers. It is at this point that the ascent becomes quite steep. There is no bus to take: One must go either by foot or by pony. Though the trek is difficult, it is also marvelous to see the waterfalls descending gracefully on either side of the path. Stark mountains all around us were dotted with tiny temples and friendly, warm *chatti*s, or rest places, refreshing to tired limbs. The chattis were set on barren ground, but were surrounded by fields of alpine flowers of every shade of color, which stretched out on both sides of the way. The U-shape of the Mandakini Valley suggests that it once contained an enormous glacier, which has since melted away.

We reached Kedarnath at noon, tired but very happy. The Kedarnath Shrine stands facing the Mandakini Valley against a background of majestic, snow-covered peaks. It is one of the twelve most sacred places dedicated to Shiva. The simple shrine, made of stone, stands on a ridge at a height of 11,500 feet.*

After making our *pronam*s (prostrations) at the sacred temple, I decided to visit the revered and highly advanced Swami Phal Hari Baba. Because of the winter snows, he ate food only from the end of April to the middle of November, while the mountain passes were open and it could be brought to him. Even so, he ate only one fruit a day, in the afternoon.

I asked him what he ate during the winter months. He replied, simply, "Air. When a yogi goes into deep meditation," he explained, "he never thinks of food and clothing. God takes care of his needs. If one is anchored in the Divine, what else does he need?"

Finally he blessed us with this timeless counsel: "Love God. Do not hate any religion, or any person.

---

*The reader will have noted that at certain places I have given the measurements in feet, and at others in meters. The reason is that, with India's comparatively recent change to the metric system, I am obliged to "straddle the fence." Some of the measurements I knew already, according to the older system. Others I have had to look up in modern guidebooks.

Do violence to no one. Give protection to all God's creatures. Meditate deeply, and in time you will see wonderful results!"

After three nights we started for Badrinath, where the famous Badrinarayan Temple sits at 12,000 feet. We spent our first night at Joshi Math, home of the semi-pastoral Indo-Mongolian people. Here stands a large ashram dedicated to Shankaracharya, for it was here that he attained enlightenment seated under a mulberry tree, which was near his cave. Atop that cave there is a tree which has been there for 2,400 years. Its girth is 125 feet!

Only nineteen miles to go! As I had obtained a pass from the Indian Government to cross the heavily guarded Manna Pass, fifteen miles from Badrinath, we had no trouble getting to the Badrinarayan Temple the next morning. However, even in these magnificent surroundings of beauty and remote stillness, the world insisted on intruding! Halfway there we had to stop while the army blasted open a mine! It was noon finally when we reached our temple destination.

Badrinath is considered the supreme pilgrimage spot for Hindus. God Himself, it is believed, lives there in human form as Badrinarayan. Shiva promised the goddess Lakshmi that he would preserve the valley of Badrivan as a place of silence and meditation, without intrusion from worldly pursuits. The shrine is fifty feet tall, and stands on the very bank of the Alaknanda River. Its façade is multicolored and painstakingly ornamented: Truly, it is a labor of love. The temple commands a majestic view of the Alaknanda, which the imagination thinks of as praising God joyfully with a musical roar. One can almost intuit what the great yogis feel who come here for meditation. The vibrations are not only deeply peaceful, but convey an all-pervading sense of actual gaiety!

In the afternoon we went behind the temple, and there met several swamis. One of these was in *maun* (silence); one was in *samadhi*; a third invited us to meditate with him, and talked to us some, mostly of God. He advised us, "Think of God as your very own Father, Mother, and Friend. Pray to Him for everything you need. God is pleased above all when you meditate and concentrate on Him. That is the way to reach His abode. Without meditation, you will have a long wait!"

The next morning I left for the Manna Pass, which took us three hours by foot. Four times I had to show my travel pass, as this entire area was under strict army control. Our way took us along the Indian side, but across from us lay China. We straggled bravely down Nil Kanta mountain, aware of Indian watchtowers everywhere.

After reaching the pass I saw a swami taking his bath at a hot springs near by. I took a bath there also, greeting him. "I have come for your *darshan*," I said. After our baths, he asked me to follow him. Soon we reached his large cave. A fire blazed inside in a deep pit. We sat around the warmth of the flames and meditated for four hours on Lord Shiva. This great yogi took no food for nine months of the year, rarely spoke, and spent most of his time in *samadhi*. He seldom emerged from his cave except to bathe in the hot springs.

As we were leaving to proceed back to Badrinath, I pronamed and said, "Baba, will you bless me?" By way of a reply he said:

"You see the Alaknanda below us? It flows from Nil Kanta on its way to the ocean—such a long way away! What tremendous love she must have for the ocean! It takes so long to reach it, but no one can stop her owing to the force of her love. Your love for God should be like that: patient, constant, unde-terred. Like a mighty river, the force of divine devo-tion will wash away any obstructions on your way. Keep on, with love, until you reach God's ocean."

I walked quickly now, because I wanted to reach the Badrinarayan Temple before dark. Once again, however, the army patrols kept stopping me to check my pass. Finally, as I was nearing my destination, a tall, robust-looking officer said to me, "Come to my office." I protested, "But Sir, I have a pass!" It didn't matter; he insisted I follow him anyway. As I sat in a chair in his office—this was certainly a change in scenery!—my mind was on Lord Shiva.

The officer asked me where I was from. "From Bengal," I said. With a great laugh he said, "I am very happy to see someone all the way from Bengal!" He then took me to his bedroom and asked someone to bring me a cot. He served me with delicious tea and snacks, then started talking about his life in the army.

He said he'd spent a few months in a Chinese jail. As he described it, it didn't strike me as being at all a good place to stay! I rose then, to continue on my journey, but he said, "No, stay here tonight as my guest." We had a delicious meal. The following morning he asked someone to drop me off at the temple gate.

Having had a most memorable experience in these sacred mountains, we returned to Joshimath, Rudra Prayag, and Karna Prayag, spending forty-five days on foot in reaching Vasistha Guha (cave), fifteen miles short of Rishikesh. This was the first time I had not made the journey to Vasistha Guha from the high mountains by bus.

Swami Purushottamananda, well-known as "the sage of Vasistha* Guha," had been living here for many years. Dr. K.M. Munshi wrote about him: "He is, I discovered, a deep Vedantin and his ways are simple, innocent, almost childlike; he smiles and smiles all the time. Loneliness, starvation, and a hundred aches and pains mean nothing to him; he lives a real life, possessed by God, who gives him perpetual joy and peace. He has attained this state after years of sadhana."

Swami Purushottamananda had become a disciple of Swami Brahmananda of Belur Math. The

---

*Vasistha was a well-known *rishi* in ancient times. He is believed to have lived here.

saint's ashram had been constructed near the original cave, in which swamis had lived for centuries. He himself had lived in it for thirty-eight years. Now sixteen disciples lived with him. He was a spiritually powerful swami and, as an extra bonus, he had a wonderful sense of humor.

The first time I visited him, his twelve large hill dogs, with faces like lions, came charging up, barking loudly and, I admit, scaring me a little. "Swamiji!" I shouted. "What is this? I've come to see you, only to be attacked by these dogs!"

He laughed merrily, then consoled me, "Don't worry. They only want to lead you to me. They love you! That's why they've come to you." His dogs were his beloved pets. The only thing he objected to in them was that they insisted on going into the cold Ganges water just outside his cave, and catching fish! Barking at guests was all right with him, and only a manifestation of their natural exuberance, but he did not like their eating fish. I wondered if certain of his guests had questioned whether eating people might have met with his approval!

I was staying at the guest house nearby. One night he asked me to come and meditate with him in his cave at midnight. I went gladly. After a time, however, I couldn't help being conscious of the loud sounds of the jungle night: tigers, dogs, and other wild creatures. Swamiji said to me, "You hear those noises? Listen to them. Try to hear Om in them, and you find you go deep into meditation." We meditated the whole night. What an advanced soul this swami was! I felt deeply privileged to spend time with him. He was a great man of God.

## Chapter Seven

# Pilgrimage to South India

After spending a few days in Delhi, we traveled south. At Madras we visited many temples, then left for the island of Rameshwaram, crossing the ocean waters by train. Here stands a very large Shiva temple, one of the most important temples in the south. Its construction was started in the 12th century, but it has been added to in subsequent centuries. Its magnificent corridors are lined with finely carved pillars. One of these corridors is 4,000 feet long!—the longest in India.

The twenty-six mile trip back to Madurai, from where we'd departed, landed us near the huge temple to Divine Mother, *Meenakshi*. It sits on fifteen acres of land. Its beautifully carved and painted gods, goddesses, and animals completely cover the nine-story-high (150 feet!) gate; it is truly awesome. Thousands of pilgrims come daily to see it, and to worship Divine Mother's *murti* there.

After two days we left for *Kanyakumari,* the southernmost tip of India, where the Bay of Bengal,

71

the Arabian Sea, and the Indian Ocean all converge. There is a wonderful memorial there, built to commemorate the spot where Swami Vivekananda went to meditate before his departure for the West to share the great teachings of India. As the foremost disciple of Sri Ramakrishna Paramhansa, Vivekananda had been invited to attend a World Parliament of Religions, planned for the following year in Chicago.

We also visited a special memorial to Gandhi, which enshrines a portion of his ashes. Finding it very peaceful here, we stayed and meditated a long time.

I had met Gandhi personally in January, 1947, when for two weeks the patrol unit I was with was told to go to a nearby village as part of the St. John Ambulance unit. Sixteen of us boys from Ashutosh College had first joined the rescue and relief efforts at the time of the Hindu-Muslim riots from August, 1946, to August, 1947.

Mahatmaji told us one evening, "Keep faith in God. Always tell the truth. Do *japa* (calling repeatedly to God in the mind) of Ram Nam all the time. And live fearlessly. Be aware that Lord Rama is always with you. He will protect you. You might die today, or live another hundred years: You cannot know. So do your duty faithfully, always thinking of Him. That is my own practice. May Ram's blessings be on you all."

Then he sang one of his own favorite songs: "*Ragupati Raghava Raja Ram, Patita Pavana Sita*

*Ram. Ishwara, Allah Tere nam: Sabko Sunmati de Bhagavan!"* Then he went into silence.

We saw him every afternoon after our rescue work for the day was finished. Every day he talked and sang, and we repeated our evening prayers together.

Many politicians would come, Muslim, Hindu: All were welcome. He emanated divine love, and also power. "If you always speak the truth," he would say, "God's power within you will increase."

\* \* \* \* \*

Formerly I had met a swami at the Kanyakumari Temple who told me the local people called him "the Pistol Swami," because he kept a pistol with him at all times! He gave me his home address, saying that if ever I returned there he would let me stay with him. He was an ex-Major General of the Indian Army. After his return from duty in Badrinarayan, he had joined the swami order through the Rama-krishna order at Belur Math. Later I saw him also during my trek to Kedarnath.

Now here I was again in Kanyakumari. After taking a bath in the ocean, I asked a young boy if he knew where the Pistol Swami was. He took me to his ashram. The swami greeted me, and we talked about my Himalayan pilgrimage.

I then added that this was probably my last visit here, as I was getting older and no longer found trekking so easy as it once had been for me. He put me up in a house near the ocean, where I slept until 2 at night. Suddenly I awoke, aware of someone moving about in the room. I began to perspire with apprehension. I could make out no form, and no one answered when I called. Drinking a glass of water, I lay down again, and, finally, slept.

After another hour, I awoke once more with a jolt. My cot was shaking! Evidently a spirit of some kind was in the room, dashing about and knocking on the door and the windows. I sat up and assumed *vajrasana* (the firm pose). Addressing the spirit in a firm voice, I said, "Hello!" as loudly and courageously as I could. "Accept my love and *pronam*s. I plan to stay here another five days. If my presence disturbs you, make a sound. If it doesn't, be quiet! I will pray for you all, and tomorrow I will do a puja at the Kanyakumari Temple for you for the salvation of your souls." From then on, they kept quiet, giving me no more trouble.

Early the next morning I went to the temple for puja. As I was performing the holy rite, a *pujari* (priest who performs sacred rites) asked me, "Are you staying at the Pistol Swami's guest house?" I replied, "Yes, I am."

"No one has been able to stay in that house, because of the presence of evil spirits." I didn't tell him I was doing puja for those very spirits!

I returned to my room at eight o'clock that morning, and found the swami gazing at my door. It dawned on me, then, that this swami was responsible for what was going on in my room! But I decided not to let him see me distressed—or fearful, as some had been—to the point of cutting my visit short.

"Namo Narayan, Swami," I said, giving him the traditional greeting of monks when they address one another. He was astonished to see me so calm.

"Did you sleep well?" he asked, gazing at me intently.

"Oh, yes." He was watching me searchingly to see my reactions. He then asked me if I would like something to eat. Not liking the fellow, I refused, as graciously as I could, then closed my door and meditated. (I never did accept food from him, as to do so would have been a signal of respect and also tacit indication that I condoned what he was doing.) To Master I prayed, "Please keep me safe!" I had a long meditation, and finally regained my strength. I had taken no food, but at least I knew that I would be all right.

That night the spirits gave me no trouble, and I rested well. Later someone told me that three persons had been killed in that house: a military man and two women. The swami was sure I was not telling him the truth about having slept well, but he didn't know what to say about it. In time I understood that this was a trick he played on guests who came for lodging, thinking to scare them, and perhaps—who knows?—even to wait and see if some of them might die of terror. He was that sort of character.

I stayed there five full nights. When I was on the

point of leaving, the swami asked me, "Did you sleep well?"

"Like a log!" I replied.

I then returned to Madurai and Madras, and eventually got back to Calcutta. I thanked our gurus all the way home for keeping me safe.

## Chapter Eight

# A Yogi Encounters Modern Science

In the year 1960, while I was again staying with Kailash Pati in Ranikhet, he told me about his guru, Narayan Swami, and suggested I travel to meet him at Vard Court Hill, sixty miles away. I decided to make the trip. For three days I walked all alone, and had no food, only water. On my way to see Narayan Swami, I stopped at Pando Kholi Hill to see a renowned swami in the area named Pahari Baba. This saint was over 150 years old!

When I reached Pahari Baba's tiny hut, I saw three people from the West talking to him. They had him hooked up to an electro-encephalograph (EEG), which traces the changes in electric patterns in the brain. They also tried repeatedly to take photographs of him with their cameras, but the shutter, which, up till then, had been working flawlessly, wouldn't work. Finally they pleaded, "Please, Swamiji, let us take at least one photo!"

Swamiji then said, "You told me that your science is 'top notch'—at the leading edge of modern technology. But I say to you, India's yoga science is far above that. And what have you been able to accomplish here?

"Well," he continued, "all right. You may take one photograph only." Thus, they were able to do so—one only!

They then asked him please to sit still, so that they might get a reading of his brain waves. "Well," he said smiling, "try it if you like." We looked at the screen only to find the lines dancing about as if in glee! The patterns should have been moving up and down at an even rate. Obviously, this swami was having fun with them.

"This shows you how far behind the yoga science you are, with your toys!" he told them happily, noting their astonished faces.

In a final attempt to get a clear picture of the brain waves of this most unusual man, they asked him, "Please, allow us one more time to see your brain moving—but in a regular pattern!" Swamiji laughed and said, "All right." He entered a trance state. Not a sign! Not a brain wave at all!

The scientists were astounded. "How is this possible?" they cried. Swamiji answered, "I was not in my body that time; therefore, there were no waves. Practice yoga, and you too will eventually be able to reach this state."

He made a further comment: "Your science can destroy life and demolish material objects. The yoga science can destroy, then re-create them at will." He continued, "For example, look at that tree. I can burn it to ashes, then give it back its life as before. Your science cannot do that. Study yoga! Our science not only gives results; it is also of practical benefit to the world.

"You are studying effects," he concluded. "What you must do is study causes." The men asked him to bless them; he replied, "The Lord will bless you."

I stayed there one hour. I told him then about Kailash Pati, and said that I was on my way at his instruction to see Narayan Swami. First, however, I asked him for a few words of spiritual advice. He told me to meditate every day, and to think of God always, putting Him first in everything I did.

"Do Kriya three or four times a day," he added, "and think of the Divine at your *Kutastha* (spiritual eye) at the point between your eyebrows. Speak the truth always; hate no other religion, for all are the same."

He gave me this illustration of the truth that is central to all religions: "If you place a red light bulb in an electric socket, it will appear red. If you replace it with a yellow one, it will appear yellow. A blue one in the same socket will appear blue. The electric power itself has no color, but its appearance changes according to its outward manifestation. God, you see, cannot be merely defined—as those scientists would like to do! He must be realized.

"God bless you," he concluded. "Divine Mother bless you." I left at noon on the fourth day for Narayan Swami's ashram (located in a place called Bharat Codé) in a greatly uplifted state of mind.

When I arrived there, Narayan Swami made the unwelcome announcement that there was no room there for me, and that I must leave. I persisted.

"Namo Narayan," I said. "I am coming from your disciple, Kailash Pati Maharaj. It was he who sent me to you." The saint studied me for a few moments, then concluded, "All right, come in." I touched his feet, and he blessed me, then gave me a small room to stay in. He himself had eaten nothing for six days, as the nearest place to obtain anything was ten miles down the mountainside. He didn't consider it worth his while to travel so far merely for food!

I talked to him about Master. He listened attentively, then said, "Men like that come to earth from the stars (that is, from infinite consciousness), when God wants them here to teach those who will listen."

I had grown sleepy. Swamiji said, "Go take rest. But do not come out of your room after midnight. Many tigers pass this way." After midnight I looked out of my window, and saw ten or twelve tigers and their cubs playing with Swamiji on the ashram grounds! As they started to pass near my hut, Swamiji told them, "Don't go near there!" They stopped at once. Swamiji then patted them like kittens. At dawn the following day, after Swamiji and I had meditated together, I asked him if I might come that evening and pat the tigers, too. For, I said, I also loved them.

Swamiji looked at me and said, "Yes, you have

80

love, but only 60%. You must increase your love another 40%. Then you can pat tigers. Otherwise they will make you into a sandwich! Tonight, however, you can watch again from your window."

At midnight the same thing happened: The tigers came; Swami came out of his room and talked to them, then he patted them while they rolled at his feet like adoring cats. Swamiji found that some of them had brought him a few rabbits to eat. He scolded them, saying to take them away. "Don't bring me fresh kills," he admonished them. At this, they slowly turned away, as if regretting the scolding, and left.

The next morning I asked the swamiji, "How is it possible for you to do that, and not for me? I love them much as I would pets. I so wanted to come out of my room while watching you with them! But I had to obey your orders." He answered, "Love is a very strong power. With love you can do anything you want. But, my dear, you must increase that power in yourself. Love God and Guru. In time, you too will be able to do anything you want."

On the third day there, someone came to receive formal blessings from Swamiji, and brought him many delectable foods for which we were very grateful. I ate with Swamiji, and he blessed me. Soon after that I left the ashram for Ranikhet, then back to Delhi.

Upon arriving in Delhi, I again went to Anandamoyee Ma's ashram. So many devotees were surrounding her! But she recognized me in the crowd and said, "How are you? Come and sit near me." Then she started singing, "Haré Krishna, haré Krishna, Krishna Krishna, haré, haré! Haré Ram, haré Ram, Ram Ram, haré, haré!" What blissful days those were!

She told me to come to her Vindhyachal ashram, near Benares, in approximately three months' time. She said she would tell a disciple to call me and let me know when she was there.

## Chapter Nine

# Fright from a Cobra!

In April 1962, Durgama, Sister Sailasuta, and Eugene Benvau, all of them members of SRF, came to Calcutta—Sailasuta for the second time. Durgama used to call me her "little brother." Sailasuta did so also. I accompanied them to Puri. After four days we returned to Calcutta, then flew on to Ranikhet to visit Babaji's cave.

Durgama, being elderly, couldn't travel up to the cave, so I took them all to visit a saintly woman called Rani Ma in the southernmost village outside of Ranikhet. (This woman is not to be confused with the earlier one of the same name, the fortune teller.) Durga Ma was very happy to meet Rani Ma, for she had heard what an affectionate, devoted, and spiritually advanced soul she was. Rani Ma had lived at this one spot for thirty years, never leaving her hut, but only meditating and communing with her Beloved in the form of Lord Krishna.

Eugene Benvau was forced to return to America for his health, so we all went back with him to New Delhi. Then, the rest of us, along with Dr. Naidoo, a newly arrived SRF devotee from Natal, South

Africa, traveled on to Benares to visit the home of Lahiri Mahasaya.

I loved Benares. Here I came often to see my good friend, Satya Charan Lahiri, the great yogi's grandson. Satya Charan lived close to the ancestral home of his grandfather and guru, and had great love for him. He adhered very strictly to the teachings, taught everyone who wanted what he had to give, and did his best to spread the Kriya Yoga teachings in his city. He was a calm and gentle man. Though I saw him many times, I never once heard him raise his voice in anger or seem unsettled—except, possibly, at the annoyance of hundreds of monkeys! They invaded his home, and his private shrine to Lahiri Mahasaya, constantly. Shibendu, his son and successor, finally placed a netting over the courtyard. So the perennial invasion of monkeys has ceased at last! Although even to this day, you can hear them chattering wildly all around the area.

We went from Benares to spend six days with Anandamoyee Ma at Vindhyachal. Here, in this peaceful place, I nearly lost my life.

Vindhyachal is sixty miles southeast of Benares. Owing to its location high in the hills, with inadequate access through dense forests, very few devotees ever go there. For this very reason, it was one of my favorite haunts. I could be with Ma there many times a day, and—added advantage!—in a less crowded setting.

On this particular visit I stayed at a small guest house about ten minutes' walk from the main ashram, where everyone else was staying. One afternoon I was eagerly looking forward to our evening darshan with Ma, had just stepped outside, and was on the point of closing the door, when a huge rat dashed by me into the hut. I had no time to go in and get him out, as it was getting late and I wanted to be present for Ma's appearance.

I was just closing the door, and turned around. To my horror, a monstrous hill cobra, called *sankhachur,* fifteen feet long, was coming straight towards me. I realized immediately that this snake had been chasing the rat. I was keeping it from its dinner! It didn't stop, but slithered along the ground, very slowly now, until it reached a point only a few feet away from me. My first thought was, "Ma, I may never get to see you again!" Then I remembered that one of the swamis in the Himalayas had given me a few tips on how to save myself if a cobra ever attacked. Remembering his advice, I slowly pulled the shawl from around my shoulders, prepared to use it as a net, if need be.

The fearsome creature began to spread its hood, getting ready to strike me. Its hissing sounds grew louder and louder, a ploy that, I knew, was intended to frighten me into running away. Certain death would attend any poor fellow who thought he could make a break for it! As this *lila* (divine play) was going on, I heard voices approaching down the path, and what sounded like people running. I was standing very still, hardly breathing, but waiting for the cobra to come close enough so that I could take my shawl and quickly wrap it around its head—where-upon I'd run for my life! (This was what the swami had told me to do, and I knew of no other way now to escape.)

Just then, out of the corner of my eye, I saw the ashram watchman coming. He had been doing his rounds of the buildings to check on them, as he did from time to time. I noticed in his hand a very large Nepali "chopper," or, as it is called, a *rambahadur.* The cobra was so wholly focused on me, however, furious at my intrusion between itself and that rat, that it didn't see the watchman slowly, slowly approaching behind it. The man motioned to me silently not to move, nor to indicate in any way that I knew he was coming. My heart was racing. Sweat was pouring down my face. I prayed to Ma with all the fervor I could muster. "Do you want me to die like this? I'm willing to, if you wish. But somehow I don't believe you do. Please interfere, then. Other-wise, both I and the watchman will surely die."

Suddenly I saw that *rambahadur* come slashing down on the cobra's neck with furious force. The cobra's head rolled ten feet down the path, and the watchman also rolled a good distance from the sheer force of his blow! The cobra's head twitched for another ten minutes. Both of us knew we mustn't come near it, for even after a cobra's head has been severed from its body its bite can be lethal.

We were both stunned, and for some time could barely move. In a matter of seconds, however, six people from the ashram came running up excitedly, asking what had happened. I said to them, "How could you know to come here just at this moment?" They replied in worried tones, "Mother said you were in danger."

Tears poured down my cheeks. How grateful I was! Even today, so many years later, I am awe-stricken at the omnipresent consciousness and the great love of this holy woman.

That night, people were gathered, telling their own favorite cobra stories. Ma knew many such stories, and related them with great glee and animation. Later, however, she said to me quietly, "Don't talk about what happened earlier. It will only frighten people. Let us sing and meditate, and try to forget it. Tonight when you return to your cabin, meditate longer than usual." I returned to my room about 9 p.m. The local government staff had cleaned the area thoroughly with carbolic acid and powder. I did not tell the rest of our party anything about it. Only Durgama came to know of it from some of the local people, and mentioned it to Sailasuta. When Sailasuta asked me what had happened, I made light of the matter, saying, "Oh, just a little snake came, but the watchman killed it. It was nothing."

Her eyes grew as big as saucers, she was so frightened. "A s-s-sna-a-a-ake??!" I knew then that Ma had been right that I should say nothing to anybody.

The next morning I left my room to have Ma's darshan before 9 a.m. She was singing. After a time she stopped to bless each one of us. We watched then for a time as she entered a state of *samadhi*.

After that we chanted Haré Krishna quietly. I thought, "She is Silence itself!"

After a while Ma opened her eyes, and looked straight at me. She asked, "How are you, Baba? Are you all right?"

"Yes, Ma, I am fine." She then advised me, "Please chant before you go to sleep tonight." I was overwhelmed by her loving concern for me.

I had asked her earlier what she thought of Durga Mata. With a blissful smile she replied, "She is floating in bliss! Her heart is full of love for God and Guru."

Later that day, when we returned to the ashram, she said to us, "I will tell you another story about a cobra.

"When I was very young, we lived in a village near Dacca. One day I was shown in a vision that it was my brother and sister's karma to die that night of a cobra bite. Immediately I went out and found two small kittens, which I placed in a basket near my brother's bed. Around midnight, while they were asleep, a cobra did indeed come into the room, headed straight for my brother and sister, then, seeing the kittens lying there within such easy reach, bit them, instead. My brother and sister were not harmed at all. The next morning I prayed for the kittens and buried them with special care."

At this point I interrupted Ma, "Will they get a human body in their next life?" Mother looked at me and laughed, then replied lovingly, "Yes, Baba, yes!"

The following day Ma told us another story. "I knew that the fifteen-year-old son of a devoted couple, who come to this body, was destined soon to die from a snake bite. I also knew that in his next incarnation he would be a great yogi and live in the Himalayas. When I told the father, he cried out, 'Please, Ma, save him! My wife and I offer his life at your feet.'

"I answered, 'Very well, but afterwards he will no longer live with you. He will go to the Himalayas and become a great yogi. That next stage will not be for family life. If you agree, then his life can be saved.' They begged me in any case to do everything I could.

"One day I was coming from Benares to this ashram with a large group of people, including Bholanath, my husband, and also this devotee couple and their son. We were walking on the slippery stone path leading to the ashram. Most of the group had gone on ahead; only a few remained behind. I was walking more slowly. All at once a large cobra appeared on the path by my foot. I asked the devotees' son to come forward and walk directly behind me. Just then, the cobra attacked, biting *me* on the foot! I then told the boy, 'You have just been saved from the death that was meant for you. Now you will have to accept a new life in the Himalayas. For you have now died, in a sense, and have been reborn.

"'Within a year,' I continued, 'you will go there and live with your guru. He will teach you the

89

wonders of God.' What could the boy say? The promise had already been given by his parents. They, in utter gratitude, said to me, 'Ma, he is yours now. Please look after him.' That evening I ate very hot kitchuri."

I said to Ma at this point in her story, "Ma, you must have been in *samadhi* not to have died." She didn't answer, but later told us that if ever one is bitten by a cobra or any other venomous creature, to eat something very hot immediately. It will help to keep the poison from harming you until medical aid can be reached. What happens is that hot milk, or hot, spicy foods slow the flow of blood to the heart, where the poison can kill you. This is only a temporary procedure, of course, useful in some cases until one can get medical attention.

One rainy evening, Ma was chanting when all of a sudden she stopped and called to an assistant. "Please get two asana blankets, and some water and sweets." Shortly afterward we heard people coming up the path chanting, "Jai Mata! Jai Mata!" Ma was pleased to see two of her well-loved swamis enter the room. "We have come from the Himalayas," they said, "on purpose to see you." Ma told them, "God bless you. Here are a few things I have put aside for you." No one had told her they were coming; she simply knew.

One of the visitors, Gopinath Babu, had been a famous lecturer at one of the large Hindu colleges. He was a very close devotee of hers. They took the sweets and water, then asked Ma, "Could you please tell us that story about 'What is God's food, and what is His duty?'" She replied with a smile, "You know it very well." But they pleaded, "Ma, please tell us anyway." Ma closed her eyes for a few moments, then began the tale.

"There was a king who wanted to know if anyone in his kingdom could answer four questions: What does God eat? Why does God weep? What makes God laugh? And what actions does God perform? He announced far and wide that whoever could answer these questions correctly within forty-eight hours would receive land, money, and his daughter's hand in marriage.

"Many learned men and sages came. None, however, could answer even one of these questions. Needless to say, the king was not happy, and those who'd entered the competition went home disappointed.

"There was a village boy tending his crops nearby. He noticed many people coming to the city with hopeful looks, then returning again wearing dour expressions. Finally the boy asked one of them, a pundit, 'Why are all of you so unhappy?' The pundit explained that the king had put them questions that no one was able to answer.

"The boy then asked, 'What were the questions?' The pundit explained them to him. The boy then exclaimed, 'Why, that's easy! If the king will accept me, I will answer his questions at once.' The pundit took the boy to the palace. On beholding the boy, young and ill clad, the king was puzzled, and

demanded to know why he had come. He little sus-
pected that this unschooled lad, after the failure of
so many great scholars, had the answers he sought.

"At the boy's insistence, the king said, 'Very well:
What does God eat?' Without hesitation the boy
answered, 'God eats the human ego. For nothing
that man identifies as his remains with him for long.
Only God is eternal.'

"The king was astonished. He liked this answer.
Next he asked, 'What makes God laugh?' The boy
replied, 'He laughs when he sees two brothers fight-
ing each other for money, land, and worldly recognition, without realizing that He himself is their only
Sustenance.'

"Surprised at the boy's wisdom, the king continued, 'All right, then, Why does God weep?' The boy
replied:

"'God comes to us four times in life to remind us
that He is always with us and guiding us, if we'll
listen to Him. He weeps when he sees how little we
care for Him.

"'The first time He comes is while we are children. He asks, "Won't you give a thought to Me?
Won't you give Me your love?" "Not just now," we
say, restlessly fidgeting. "We are too busy with toys
and our other playthings."

"'God comes to us a second time after we grow
up. He asks, "Now won't you think of Me? Won't
you give Me your love?" "Oh, I'm busier than ever
now!" we reply with anxious frowns. "I have a job,
a wife, always more children! Later, Lord, later."

Sadly then, God says, "All right. I won't insist, since that is your desire."

"'God comes to us a third time in life as we are growing old, and asks us again, "Now, at last, won't you love Me?" But we respond, our eyes unhappy and our shoulders bowed with care, "Oh, I'd love even a little peace! But my son is getting married. My daughter needs a husband. My wife is ill." God says then, as if with tears, "I understand. I will return and ask you one more time."

"'Soon we are old. Our children have left us, and no longer care much about us. Our wives nag us for things we can't give them. We ourselves are ill. God would still come to us, and tries to. But our minds are too heavy, filled with regrets for the past and sighs for what might have been if only things had turned out differently. God stands waiting, and asks us to remember Him at least at the time of death. But we can't see Him, for habit has fixed our eyes to the ground.

"'And so, death comes, and God says, "My dear child, I have other lives, including your next one, to tend to now. I came to you many times, but every time you refused me. What can I give you now but my tears?"'"

"The king, extremely impressed with the boy's answers, posed his fourth and last question: 'What actions does God perform?' The boy sat there, and said nothing. The king, puzzled, said, 'You came here claiming you could answer all four of my

93

questions. Now you sit there, silent. Don't you know the answer?'

"'I know it,' the boy replied, 'but I cannot give it to you from where I am sitting.' The king asked, 'Where must you be, to respond?' The boy replied, 'I must be seated on your throne. Only then can I answer you. Meanwhile, your Majesty, you yourself must be here on the floor where I am.'

"The king's curiosity was so aroused that he agreed to this condition, and allowed the boy to sit on his own throne, while he himself sat on the floor below him. He then repeated his question: 'What actions does God perform?'

"'He performs no action, directly,' replied the boy. 'Everything He does is performed through creatures like you and me. See? now you are a village boy, and I am—temporarily—your king. Such is the nature of life: endlessly changing. One day, a person sits on high; the next day, he is plunged in poverty. Neither state is permanent, and neither is better or worse than the other. Thus God helps man to understand that everything is His play.

"'What does God do, then? Nothing! For, on the one hand, nothing exists but Himself, His love and bliss. The universe is His dream. At the same time, however, in His dream he can produce whatever He chooses, for He, in fact, does everything. Thus, with God nothing is impossible!'"

The following morning the two swamis left for their home in the Himalayas. Mother told me later that they were very advanced souls, and that they seldom came down from their forest abode. Before their departure I had a chance to talk with them personally for a few moments. They embraced me and said, "Hold the rope tightly; don't lose it! One day, if you cling to the thought of God, He will pull you up into His light."

I once asked Ma, "If I were to stay in the mountains for long periods of seclusion, where should I go to be near highly advanced souls?" Two days passed before I received her response. Then she said, "You will not live in the mountains in this incarnation. Soon you will marry. In your next life, however, you will live close to those you would like to be with now."

Another time I asked Ma, "Would you be willing to give me the address of at least one great Himalayan yogi?" She looked at me deeply, then said, "Oh, Baba, you still have so much work to do as a father and husband. As a Truth seeker, you will come across many spiritual aspirants of all types. You must learn to see God in all of them, the bad as well as the good. Follow the good ones, and blessings will be yours. God and Guru will guide you. My blessings also are with you." Even today, I take her words as a lifeline.

After Hassi and I were married, I took her to see Ma in Benares. In fact, the last two times I saw Ma were in that holy city in the company of Hassi and our son Manash. She told me I was performing a great duty, and that I should be fully satisfied with my life. She was happy to see us, and blessed us, saying to come frequently.

"Always keep in mind that you are fulfilling your God-appointed duty, and are therefore pleasing to Him. Try to finish your karma by doing nothing wrong, and by offering everything up to Him. Finally, reflect on the value of silence. Try to talk a little less!" I vowed that I would do all that she had asked of me.

I bow my head at Anandamoyee Ma's holy feet. She lived from 30th April, 1896 to 27th August, 1982, leaving her body at Kankhal, near Haridwar, in the Uttar Pradesh province of India. Hers was one of the most glorious lives of our times. All my pronams to this great woman saint, and mother of Bengal!

## Chapter Ten

# God in Organizations: God in Our Souls

Later that same year, 1961, Dayama returned to India with Mrinalini Mata and Ananda Mata, both of them members of the SRF board of directors. (Kriyananda had already returned a year earlier after an absence in America of seven months.) Dayama was very happy to see me, and I too was overjoyed. At the same time, I was anxious to discuss with her a certain problem we were encountering in our YSS work in India.

Many Indian saints through the centuries, including not a few of those mentioned in this book, have spoken a little disparagingly of spiritual organizations. Their disaffection is understandable. For one thing, as saints I have known have said repeatedly, meditation is the right and true way to know God. Meditation, however, is also a personal and private practice. It cannot be improved by institutional control.

Anandamoyee Ma, about whom I have written repeatedly in these pages, never associated herself mentally with the organization that her disciples had lovingly built in her name. Even when disciples came to consult her about some article that had appeared in their magazine, she replied, "It is *your* magazine!"

Yet much good also has been done by spiritual organizations. For example, they provide *Satsanga* (good company), which all the scriptures highly recommend. They can assist in spreading the spiritual teachings. And they offer to those who want to live spiritually dedicated lives a means also of serving God. The negative aspects of organizations lie not so much in their outer form as in the focus they provide for various human weaknesses—frailties that are already present in the human heart, but that sometimes gain strength in group settings.

Organizations, moreover, are not an abstraction: They consist of people. Although their purpose is to help those people, the people themselves often misuse them in order to increase, rather than eliminate, their own ego-bondage. Thus, difficulties arise, and, like ripples spreading outward on a lake when a stone has been flung into it, move outward and affect everyone concerned. Thus, organizations sometimes end up becoming mere free-for-alls of competing egos!

This situation is all the more insidious because the people concerned usually disclaim any semblance of desiring power, while making an outward show of humility.

Paramhansa Yogananda accomplished a wonderful thing in founding SRF/YSS. Without it, the message of Kriya would not have been heard in the West, except possibly as a whisper. He himself was sadly aware, however, of the dangers involved in organizational work and throughout his life spoke wistfully of the simple life in the ashrams of India. He was obedient to the will of God, however, and God and his own line of gurus had told him to create an institution in America. Perhaps his very disinclination for the role of organizer helped to insure that his organization would blend the best of Western and Indian values. His fears, however, as well as his hopes have been amply realized over the years. Fortunately, because his mission was divinely ordained, the fulfillment of his hopes has greatly outweighed what the years have brought in justification for his fears.

An important question remains: Are spiritual organizations, of the Western type at least, truly beneficial for India? Swami Vivekananda thought so, but that swami's emphasis was on India's social upliftment, which was greatly needed after centuries of foreign rule—and misrule! Vivekananda was seeking a corrective for India's present condition; it was not his purpose to replace our ancient spiritual traditions. For social upliftment, moreover, Western-style organization offers indeed an excellent model to follow.

Yet India's spiritual strength has always largely

been due to the fact that its genius is for *personal* spiritual growth, not for the efficiency of a well-run institution. Indeed, when it comes to organizing, India may well be described as the land of *dis*unity. What has always been emphasized in this country is inner soul-development. This emphasis, Swami Kriyananda has interestingly remarked, is evident in the emphasis in Indian music on melody, rather than harmony, and the inability Indian musicians have displayed so far to match the subtleties of Western harmony.*

An appreciation for harmony, Kriyananda says, develops when people's thinking goes toward group activities. For group thinking to lead toward outward progress, harmony in musical expression can help to generate spiritual attitudes. On the other hand, where pleasing harmony is lacking in chord progressions, cacophony and discord result not only in the music, but in those people who expose themselves to the music. India, though it lacks the "genius" for cooperative effort (and therefore for musical harmony), has produced an extraordinary number of individual spiritual geniuses. Moreover, he says, it is individual aspiration that provides the soil in which true genius flowers.

The West has tried to ensure the purity of its spiritual teachings by organizing and controlling them. In India, however, the most refined essence of spiritual truth has been preserved. India, far more than

---

*Kriyananda has, as part of his service to Master, composed some 400 pieces of music, and has achieved some renown in this field. Hence his interest in comparing Indian and Western music.

Western civilization, has ever recognized that it is the life in a plant which produces the plant, not the plant which brings life into existence. These reflections of Kriyananda's may give a clue as to India's talent for spiritual genius, but lack of talent for spiritual organization.

It may be that our Master's work was not meant to develop in India, at least as a Western-style organization. His life mission lay in the West. Had it been in India, perhaps he would have approached it very differently—as, in fact, his *paramguru* Lahiri Mahasaya did, who asked that Kriya Yoga be spread with as little emphasis on organization as possible. On the other hand, it may be that another kind of spiritual organization altogether is destined for India's future, and that no institution would develop such as Westerners understand the word, with its corporation presidents, vice presidents, secretaries, boards of directors, and offices filled with efficient workers.

At any rate, Dayama once asked Master how his work should be developed in India. His reply to her was, "They will organize themselves."

YSS's history in India to date forces the question: "Has the Western model, even if workable in America, proved helpful in India?" The only possible answer is, "Not yet, at any rate."

Dayama found in Binay Dubey a "super-organization man" who fitted her own experience and understanding of organizations. It was natural that she should pin her hopes on him for the development of Master's work in India. Master had said to her, regarding the work in India, "They will organize themselves." Well, she must have thought, here was an Indian who could organize everything according to her own understanding of the way organizations needed to be run. This could not but strike her as an ideal way to follow her own guru's instructions. Now, the Indian work could be organized by an Indian, as Master had said, and at the same time follow the lines that she herself knew and could relate to.

Binayendra Nath Dubey was already the founder-director of Niramoy, a famous hospital in West Bengal. His organizational talents were considerable. Moreover, Dubey expressed the fullest confidence in those methods, and also in himself as a leader within that system. He was, at heart, a bureaucrat.

Swami Virajananda, a leading and life-long disciple of Anandamoyee Ma, once said to Swami Kriyananda, "At first, Dubey impressed me. Gradually, however, I've discovered that his motives are political, not spiritual. Since that time, I have kept away from him." Dubey, however, was able by his Westernized skills at organization to win Dayama's confidence.

It is unseemly to speak ill of the dead. Nevertheless, the fact must be stated that Dubey cannot have been destined for the responsibility Dayama placed on his shoulders, for he did not live to implement any of it. He visited America, where she made him a swami and gave him full authority to develop YSS according to the methods he championed. Very soon, however, after his return to India from the United States he developed cancer and not long afterward died. One naturally asks, Could his death possibly have been a divine sign that Dayama was mistaken in placing confidence in him? In fact, his death ended for the time being all of Dayama's hopes for Master's Indian work to be developed from America.

Paramhansa Yogananda knew that the true genius of India is different from America's. Each of these countries has something important to give to the other. The genius of India, particularly, lies in its dedication to inner spiritual development; of America, in outer cooperation. If a spiritual organization is ever to succeed in India, it cannot but be in an inward, not an outward, direction.

India will, I believe, concentrate on perfecting above all the inner relationship of devotee and guru. It will shrink back, as if from a cobra, at any suggestion of giving spiritual obedience to some mere official of an institution.

It is interesting, in this context, to note the very first words in Yogananda's *Autobiography of a Yogi*. "The characteristic features of Indian culture," he wrote, "have long been a search for ultimate verities and the concomitant disciple-guru relationship."

It has been stated truly by wise men and women of India that this country has fallen, of recent times, too much under the sway of "gurudom." This development is probably due to the shock of foreign, and particularly of modern, influences. At the present time, too many reputed "gurus," themselves insufficiently enlightened, have been swayed by the quest for social and political upliftment in the name of serving God, but not by the hope of inspiring people to commune more deeply with Him. This phenomenon cannot but be temporary, however. The very stones of India are permeated with a different vibration. Time surely will bring a change. The need of the devotee, however, for a true guru will never change.

I include these reflections here, not with the purpose of ending my book on a note of negative speculation, but only as a loving caution to those who, in future, recognize the advantages of spiritual organizations, but are anxious to avoid their disadvantages. From the standpoint of Master's work in India, Dayama's confidence in Dubey was—and this conclusion can hardly be avoided—unfortunate.

Dubey used his power to control people. Thus, he made many lives—my own included—miserable. I am sad for what has happened to a great and noble work, which might have brought—and which, with God's grace, could still bring—inspiration and guidance to millions, had its focus only been on love, rather than on power and on controlling others.

Anyone who wants to found an organization must keep firmly in mind that, far more important than any outward position, is the spirit of those who serve in that position. Efficiency is a minor matter compared to the spirit of love. Those doing spiritual service should love God first; then love Him in others. Nor can any organization replace the need for an enlightened guru, or at any rate a spiritually advanced teacher whose vision of truth inspires others deeply.

Dubey pretended faithfulness to the Guru. He was also, in his way, devoted to Dayama. Yet it was always devotion and loyalty according to his own understanding and definition, which he filtered through his own worldly institutionalism. He was one of those people who, by their very exuberance, get others to nod in tentative agreement with them, then draw from him professions of love and loyalty for their astuteness. Few people have the common sense to resist any snare set with such a bait, and Dubey often said of Americans that they are like "babes in the woods"— no match for the subtle cunning of the Indian mind. What this means of course is that people like Dubey themselves look on life as a contest.

Dubey had been born a *zemindar* (landowner). His attitudes strongly reflected his upbringing. It was basic to his personality to be forceful, authoritarian, and inconsiderate of others except where astute policy dictated kindness. He treated lightly such worldly usages as drinking spiritous liquors—a habit strictly forbidden to aspiring yogis. Lacking attunement with the Guru, which Yogananda is still to all who follow him, and feeling a surge of energy that came as a result of controlling others, he quickly lost the friendship and respect of all of us, an esteem which, at first, we naturally gave him.

Dayama listened to my criticisms of his actions on her return to India in 1961. It was soon evident, however, that her mind was made up. She placed Dubey on the Board of Directors of SRF/YSS, and immediately thereafter we Indians were told that we had to obey him in everything. It confused me, I confess, to see a man in charge of our organization who, not only in my opinion but in that of all those I knew, was so obviously worldly, not spiritual. Dubey's direction included managing the lives and the spiritual service of us renunciates. Our personal interest was the attainment of God-realization; we were not interested in self-aggrandizement. To him, however, we were no better than "employees"— pawns on a chessboard.

I have asked myself many times since then, Might it be that I was mistaken? Time, thus far, has not endorsed that doubt. In all fairness, however, I must also admit that forty years is a short time in the history of a work that is destined for the ages. Indeed, I should *like* to be wrong, for I believe in Master's mission, and in Dayama's faithfulness to Master as his disciple.

Needless to say, I have touched here only lightly on the events that actually occurred. Those events were painful to me. To you, the reader, they might appear merely interesting. Or—and this is my real concern—you might be discouraged by them, rather than take them as the cautionary lesson I have tried to convey.

There are many devotees, however, who have been deeply hurt. My hope is that, in writing about these things, I might turn that hurt to good effect by encouraging people's faith in spiritual, rather than in institutional, ways of seeking God. For in the case of YSS, the teachings themselves are wonderful. They need only to be offered in a way that is natural to India: whether within or outside of institutions, but always with love first for God, and for all of God's children.

For the Indian mind is subtle, yes, but in true devotees it is never so in the cunning way that Dubey described except, which is what happens, when cunning is directed toward self-aggrandizement. With the addition of ego-motivation, subtlety becomes its own undoing. In essence, however, the subtle perceptions for which the Indian mind is so notably gifted reveal the Divine Hand in everything, and open the heart in childlike wonder to the Divine Presence everywhere. Once this understanding flowers in the mind, the Kriya Yoga teachings will be able to bring hope and inspiration to millions, whether within or outside of any institution.

## Chapter Eleven

# A New Flowering?

Not long after Dayama's return to India, she went for some needed rest to Kashmir. I was invited to accompany her and her entourage. She expressed joy to be able to spend hours with me in that place of peace, free from responsibilities. Sometimes we would meditate 5–6 hours together. Though I couldn't be with her as long as I'd have liked, I've never forgotten her motherly love for me. An amusing recollection comes to mind: I taught her to chew cardamom seeds, which she greatly enjoyed. Even to this day I send her a package of them in special remembrance of the time we spent together there.

On July 1, 1961, I left again for Kashmir, this time to go to Amarnath,* where huge natural ice monuments in the forms of Lord Shiva, Durga, and Ganesha (the great elephant god) stand deeply recessed in the caves. The mountain passes are open only for the month of July, so my timing was very

---

*Amar Nath* is a name of Shiva, and means, "Deathless Lord." Today, no one can go to Amarnath without the help of the Indian army and police, because of terrorist troubles.

important. The first day Amarnath opens to pilgrims is the day in India called *Guru Purnima Day,* or the day in honor of the guru, in whatever form you accept him. (The last day is *Rakhi Purnima,* or *Raksha Bardhan.*) On reaching Kashmir I met the few friends who planned to make up our team, and the four of us began our trek. First, we took a bus to Pahalgao, then walked to Ananta Nag and Chandanbari, two small villages along the way. The mountain tracks here, known as *pisu,* border on steep, treacherous cliffs and are very narrow. They are also extremely dangerous, due partly to the fact that the views from here are so spectacular that you can get lost in their beauty and forget to watch your step! The snow-capped Himalaya, the highest mountains in the world, seem embodiments of the gods. They have so much power and aloof nobility that one is enraptured. It is very difficult to take one's eyes from them, for they make one feel that, on some level, one's own spirit belongs with them.

We climbed until late in the day, most of that time crawling on our hands and knees like insects until we reached Seshnag, where the auspicious *Panchatarani* flows. *Pancha* means "five," and at this spot five rivers converge. Next, we trekked through snow until arriving at the temple two miles further on. The villagers tell a lovely story of two doves that, they say, have always lived here. They call them Durga and Shiva.

One night the heavens opened up and engulfed us with heavy rains, and then snow. Nothing was visible around us. The winds were fierce, as though they wanted to force us off the mountain. I prayed to Master please to allow us the opportunity to see the temples dedicated to God. We returned to a place called the Silk Factory to stay for a few days, until the storm abated. At last we could move on, and visited *Khirvabani,* a Shankaracharya temple sitting high in the forest. The place was extremely beautiful, with apple orchards in full bloom, grape arbors sprinkled with crystal snows, and with a lovely, deep blue lake set in a pristine valley of wild roses and other mountain flowers. I went there twice.

* * * * *

It seemed for a time that our work might be developing a major center in New Delhi. This had all begun a year and a half previously, when I received a letter from Kriyanandaji asking me to come see him. He had been lecturing in Simla (a Himalayan hill station), Patiala (a city in Punjab), Chandigarh (the capital of Himachal Pradesh), and finally in New Delhi, and had been having major success everywhere he went. As soon as possible I joined him in New Delhi, and planned to stay there about a week. I knew certain political ministers and other New Delhi dignitaries, so he asked me if I might arrange a series of lectures and a press conference, that he might meet people who could be interested in our teachings. Thus we might see, together, how much might be done towards helping India.

We invited, among others, the law minister, Mr.

Asoka Sen; Mr. Ananda Swami Iyanger, the speaker of Parliament; and the director of Bharatiya Vidya Bhavan College, where Kriyananda would later speak, as well. I booked the Russell Hotel for the press conference because it had a large meeting hall. People were very enthusiastic. An American swami had come to Delhi! At first the interest was just that it was unusual for such a person to come and lecture to Indians. Soon, however, it became obvious that this man knew what he was talking about! He had real depth of spirit and sincerity. Everyone was thrilled to hear his lectures. Not only was he magnetic and joyful, but he understood the Indian people and talked as one of us. Thousands came to hear him—two thousand at his first lecture!—and

Kriyananda in Patiala, India

his audiences kept on growing. He always spoke of his guru, and told us that to find happiness in this world one must serve a higher Source than the little ego. His lectures were deeply moving, and the Masters' presence was felt by many there. I came for one week, and stayed for three, returning home after that, to Calcutta.

The work developing in New Delhi turned out to become a major test for our work in India, and the means through which Dubey's vision for the organization became, as it were, set in concrete.

Kriyananda, with Dayama's consent, set out to purchase a piece of property where SRF/YSS could build a retreat center for all of India. The money for this project had been promised him from two important sources. The big problem was getting the government's permission, for the land he wanted was in what is called the "green belt" area around the city, which was not available for private use. Thus, obtaining this land was not an easy assignment, yet he worked day and night to help the dream to become a reality.

Mrs. Rani Bhan and her adopted son Indu (Indra Jit) helped us immeasurably. Mrs. Bhan, a disciple of Anandamoyee Ma's from her childhood, had a friend in Indira Gandhi, the daughter of Jawaharlal Nehru, India's prime minister. Indira Gandhi helped significantly toward obtaining the land in New Delhi. Finally, Prime Minister Nehru himself walked the property in June of 1961, and gave it his personal blessing.

Unfortunately, trouble was brewing behind our backs. Shortly before Nehru gave his actual blessings, and while everyone was filled with gratitude for the many souls who were being brought to Master, rumors arose among the directors in America—originating, it seems, from Calcutta—that Kriyananda was doing all this for his own glory. It was not true, and only Master knows why this great work was denounced to, and by, the SRF directors in America. Certain it is that Dubey was unhappy to see energy being drawn away from Calcutta, and from himself.

Back now to 1961 and my return from Kashmir. On my return from there, I realized that my friends, who were the strength behind the YSS work, had grown disillusioned. All of them had left. Dubey himself also warned me, repeatedly, to be careful not to contradict him in any way.

It wasn't long after that that Atmanandaji Maharaj (who also was no longer in the work) became sick and had to be hospitalized for a month. No help came from YSS. Dubey stopped Atmananda's medical and pocket expenses, which until then had been continuing. This abrupt change led, I sincerely believe, to Atmananda's early death.

I wrote Dayama in protest, asking her why there was no money for our brothers who had worked so hard to keep this work alive, and why Dubey was responsible for all decisions in such matters now. She said she would do something about it. The next thing I knew, however, Sri Binay Dubey was made the Secretary of the Board, and nothing changed. I had a very strong talk with Dubey about his treatment of Atmanandaji, but my efforts did no good. Atmanandaji ended up staying with Tulsi Bose after he got out of the hospital. He passed away there on 17th February, 1963, having never recovered from his illness.

It was sometime later, in 1962, that Dubey told me quite smugly that SRF had telephoned Kriyanandaji at Surai Khet, a Himalayan foothill village where he was resting after his long and—as he imagined—victorious efforts to establish the work in New Delhi, and told him to come immediately to New York City. There he was met by two directors, Daya Mata and Tara Mata. To his intense agony, he was dismissed unconditionally from the work, being allowed to speak not a single word in his own defense, and with no explanation that he could even remotely accept as valid. He was warned never to contact any SRF member, either in America or in India, and never again to set foot on any SRF/YSS property. He was permitted to keep the little money he had with him, but was given no further allowance, and was left from that time on to rebuild his life as he chose. "Just take any job that comes along," was the advice given him.

This was, in fact, the prelude for the great service to his guru that Kriyananda has accomplished since then, following the instructions Yogananda himself had given him. This service had seemed to him impossible to obey in the context of SRF. His dismissal, in other words, proved not the misfortune it seemed at the time, but a miraculous blessing on his life.

Chapter Twelve

# No Tibet This Time

In 1963, soon after Swami Atmananda's death, I felt a strong desire to go to Tibet, there to meet great saints. A swami at the Sivananda ashram in Rishikesh had also wanted to go, and agreed to accompany me. So in 1963 we left on another trek, this time past the holy city of Almora just north of Naini Tal. We were never able to reach Tibet owing to China's invasion of that country. No foreigners were allowed across the Tibetan border.

In Almora, however, we met a great saint, a British man who Anandamoyee Ma told me later was a very advanced swami. His name was Krishna Prem, which means "Beloved of Krishna," and he certainly was that. For he was a great devotee, and whenever speaking, spoke only of Krishna. I asked him if he ever got lonely, living so far away from other people. "Oh no!" he said. "I am always talking to Krishna. He is dearer to me than my own self." He was like butter: soft and lovable, yet with great strength of character—like Krishna himself! He had a large statue of his Beloved, and we meditated there with him for a while. He then fed us lunch. We stayed only a couple of hours, but it was worth the entire trip. Perhaps that was Master's wish for us anyway, and not Tibet. Krishna Prem passed away in 1985. I feel blessed for the good fortune of having met him.

\* \* \* \* \*

Dayama came back to India a few more times: once in 1964 and again in 1969. In Dakshineswar, Dubey chastised me repeatedly for creating what he called "a wall of obstruction" in the work. (The rest of us knew all along that what he wanted was total control, and that it was in that ambition that he was feeling "obstructed.") He couldn't argue with me in public, though, so he simply smiled, knowing that he would "win" in the end. He refused to listen when I explained to him that Master felt it was important to keep the traditional customs in Indian ashrams, and told him he was hurting people with his ignorance and haughtiness. Daya said to me, "Why not follow him a little bit?" But what he was doing was not dharmic. If you were my superior, and said to me, "The sun rises in the West," would dharma tell me to agree with you?

Well, Dubey finally got everything he'd wanted. All the original ashram monks left including, in 1966, myself. I said to him, "Now you are happy! Because of you, Kriyananda is gone, Atmananda is gone, Paramananda is gone, Gyanananda is gone, I am gone. We are all gone. And now the work is being led by a worldly person like yourself. I thank Master for taking me out at this time, for you will be the ruin of it. I am ashamed at your total lack of respect for what Master wanted this work to be."

Swami Gyanananda and Paramananda and I have remained good friends over the years. Gyanananda I see often. At one time a devotee gave him a statue of Lord Krishna. He worshiped it every day. In 1959, when he left Calcutta and YSS for Haridwar, he asked me to keep this Krishna *murti* for daily puja worship, which I perform twice daily. Since then the *murti* has been with me. Sometimes a devotee asks to borrow him for a week or two, and I am happy to oblige. I try to go every year in June

Left: Gyanananda in Dehra Dun, 1998. Right: Krishna *murti* given to me by Gyanananda in 1959.

118

to stay with Gyanananda for a month in his lovely little hut in the hills of Mussoorie, near Dehra Dun.

Over the years Kriyananda and I have become very good friends. I have been gratified to see all that he has been able to accomplish for his guru without the "obstruction" of institutional affiliation. He has created flourishing communities, both in America and in Italy: spiritual villages, rather than monasteries, but for all that *ashram*s, where many hundreds of people live dedicated lives of service and meditation. In these ashrams there are thriving schools for children, and activities from which thousands of people receive teaching and inspiration. Here, possibly, lies a model for the kind of "institution" that could serve India in the future: not a Western, super-organized set-up as Dubey favored, but free-flowing places, filled with divine love.

In 1986, the first group of pilgrims from these Ananda ashrams in America (*Ananda* means "divine joy") came to Calcutta and visited Tulsi Bose's home. Since then the group has come eight times. How beautiful it has been to see so many devotees from America enjoy, with deepest appreciation, the places where Master lived, walked, and taught in India. I explained to them the relics in our meditation room: the stately trident of Lahiri Mahasaya's, which he gave to Sri Yukteswar, from whom it came to Tulsi Bose and has been with Hassi and me ever since; Sri Yukteswar's conch; Master's spoon, plate, knife, and cane; Anandamoyee Ma's shawl; the Krishna *murti* that Gyanananda gave to me in honor of our deep friendship in God; and many, many others.

The Ananda devotees meditated in our home for long periods of time, donated money for the remodeling of the rooms, and told me they felt as though this was their home, too.

Over the years we have become very good friends, and it was with great joy that we received an invitation in 1993 to come to Ananda Village for the 100th Anniversary of Yogananda's birth. Hassi and I, and Hare Krishna Ghosh and his wife Anjali all went joyfully to America on this Ananda pilgrimage, where we were invited also to speak. Vidura and Durga met us in New York City and accompanied us to California. In New York we visited, among other

Our meditation room

places, Carnegie Hall where Master, in April, 1926, had lectured and sung to a packed auditorium of three thousand people.

In Carnegie Hall Master had that whole crowd, most of them completely new to his teachings, enthusiastically singing with him for an hour and a half the Indian chant, "O God Beautiful!" Many miracles of healing occurred that evening, including one of a man who burst angrily into Master's interview room afterward, flung a revolver onto his desk, and cried, "I ought to shoot you for what you've done to me! I can't go back to my life of crime

Hare Krishna and Anjali Ghosh during their visit to America in 1993

anymore!" So saying, he left, leaving the revolver on the desk as a donation—a rather strange "thank you present" for his spiritual healing!

At Ananda we stayed with Brian and Lisa Powers, who took care of all our needs. We also went to Lake Tahoe and visited Los Angeles, where I fulfilled a dream of mine: visiting the Biltmore Hotel where, on 7th March, 1952, Master left his body.

We were especially blessed, in Los Angeles, to visit Master's ashrams. At Mt. Washington, SRF's headquarters ("Mother Center" it is called), we again met with Dayama, Ananda Mata, Sailasuta, Daya's brother Richard Wright (who visited India with Master in 1935), and others. We had the blessing of meditating in Master's bedroom, visited his sitting room where he used to receive guests, and meditated on the grounds where, Master told his disciples, "I have meditated in every place on this property."

We also visited the other Ananda ashrams, or "colonies," as Master called them. I had never thought I would be able to visit these holy places. I thank Master and Kriyananda for making it possible to fulfill my greatest wish, and Vidura and Durga for taking us everywhere. I deeply pray to Divine Mother for the health of these good friends, and for their ever-deepening devotion to God and Guru. I deeply pray also for Kriyananda and for his continued good health and ability to serve Master in unceasing activity and devotion. I feel that Master is behind him in all he does, and that he will be so always.

To finish our trip, we visited my old friend Paramananda in Naples, Florida, and spent ten days in his home. Paramananda is a devotee of Ma Kali, and has a large statue of Her in his meditation room. He feels particularly close to Her, as his Divine Mother. The room is filled with Her presence. May the Divine Mother deeply bless him.

Hassi and I in Calcutta during an Ananda pilgrimage in 1987

## Chapter Thirteen

# The Travelers Return

Our trip took us safely back to Calcutta on 23rd September, 1993, filled with deep and deeply joyful memories.

Rabindranath Tagore said it beautifully for me:

> Yes, I am a Traveler.
> Nothing can hold me back.
> Pleasure and pain seek to bind me,
> But, ah! my home lies far beyond.

And so ends the simple story of one devotee's quest for the Divine Beloved. Like life itself, the tale contains both sadness and joy. With God's blessings, however, the good experiences have been far more than merely "good": They have been wonderful and inspiring in the only sense that matters, the divine. The painful memories, too, leave me now with gratitude, for they have taught me important lessons that have aided me in my journey toward our eternal home—yours, mine, and every soul's.

May you, who have read this account, draw from it only blessings and hope for the future. For that is how, in retrospect, I view all that has happened to me in life. For the love and joy especially, but also for any wisdom I have gained in my travels, I am grateful beyond words.

During the Centennial Celebration of Yogananda's birth at Ananda Village in 1993. Behind me are Lisa Powers, Hare Krishna Ghosh, and Lila Hoogendyk.

# Autobiography of a Yogi

By Paramhansa Yogananda
(Reprint of the Philosophical Library 1946 First Edition)
Trade Paperback, 481 pages with photographs

*"As an eyewitness recountal of the extraordinary lives and powers of modern Hindu saints, the book has importance both timely and timeless."*
—W.Y. Evans-Wentz, M.A., D.Litt., D.Sc., Jesus College, Oxford;
Author of *The Tibetan Book of the Dead*

Followers of many religious traditions have come to recognize this book as a masterpiece of spiritual literature. Yogananda was the first yoga master of India whose mission it was to live and teach in the West. His first-hand account of his life experiences includes childhood revelations, stories of his visits to saints and masters in India, and long-secret teachings of Self-realization that he made available to the Western reader.

This highly prized verbatim reprinting of the original 1946 edition is the only one available free from textual changes made after Yogananda's death. Experience all its inherent power, just as the great master of yoga first presented it.

# The Path

## One Man's Quest on the Only Path There Is

J. Donald Walters (Swami Kriyananda) • Trade paperback 420 pages

What would it be like to live with a great spiritual master? Here, with over 400 stories and sayings of Paramhansa Yogananda, is the inspiring story of one man's search for truth. It led him to the great master's door, where he learned to live the spiritual life more perfectly through his teacher's training and example. A vitally useful guide for sincere seekers on any path. Filled with insightful stories and mystical adventures, *The Path* is considered by many as a companion to Yogananda's *Autobiography of a Yogi*.

# The Hindu Way of Awakening
## Its Revelation, Its Symbols
## An Essential View of Religion
Swami Kriyananda (J. Donald Walters) ◆ Trade paperback, 349 pages

Swami Kriyananda's inspired, entertaining, energetic writing style makes this book delightful reading for anyone interested in spirituality and the deeper meanings of religion. He brings order to the seeming chaos of symbols and deities in Hinduism, revealing the underlying teachings from which they arise, truths inherent in all religions, and their essential purpose: the direct inner experience of God. Intended for followers of all faiths—and no faith— *The Hindu Way of Awakening* will enrich your life and feed your soul.

# Awaken to Superconsciousness
## How to Use Meditation for Inner Peace, Intuitive Guidance, and Greater Awareness
J. Donald Walters ◆ Hardcover, 270 pages

Sweeping in its scope, unparalleled in its depth, *Awaken to Superconsciousness* is one of the best guides to meditation, yoga, and the spiritual path that you'll ever read. Intended for both beginners and long-time practitioners, it expertly weaves together the seemingly different pieces and practices of the spiritual path and offers a comprehensive, easy-to-understand program guaranteed to help you feel immediate, life-changing results.

# The Rubaiyat of Omar Khayyam Explained
## by Paramhansa Yogananda
Edited by J. Donald Walters ◆ Hardcover, 354 pages w/illustrations

Nearly 50 years ago, Yogananda discovered a scripture previously unknown to the world. It was hidden in the beautiful, sensual imagery of the beloved poem, *The Rubaiyat of Omar Khayyam*. His commentary unlocks the spiritual mystery of this famous poem, revealing it to be a profound and inspiring allegory of the soul's romance with God.

## Wave of the Sea
**Chants from Ananda**

Lift your heart in devotion with chants written by Yogananda and Kriyananda, as well as traditional Indian chants and mantras. These chants, beautifully sung by musicians from Ananda, are accompanied by harmonium, guitar, flute, harp, kirtals, and tabla.

## Surrender: Mystical Music for Yoga
Derek Bell and Agni

More than just beautiful background music, the instrumental selections on Surrender are chosen and arranged to mirror the normal progression of yoga routines. Release tension, enter states of deep relaxation, and heighten your awareness. Can also be used to accompany healing work or meditation.

## I, Omar
Donald Walters

Inspired by the ancient mystical poem, *The Rubaiyat of Omar Khayyam,* this haunting melody is taken up in turn by the English horn, oboe, flute, harp, guitar, cello, violin, and strings. *". . . Ahhh! I've spent many spins with this album, and never tire of the theme."*
—Carol Wright, Reviewer, *New Age Voice*

*Crystal Clarity, Publishers and Clarity Sound & Light*
**14618 Tyler-Foote Road**
**Nevada City, CA 95959-8599**

*For more information or a free catalog* **call 800-424-1055 or 530-478-7600 Fax: 530-478-7610**

*E-mail: clarity@crystalclarity.com* *Website: www.crystalclarity.com*